# CATCH the VISION, Find Your MISSION

## Written By Andrew Nelson

**Editor: Greg Kuschwara**
**Assistant Editor: Suzanne Harbord**
**Illustrator: Andrew Nelson**
**Cover Design: Anthony Smith**

ISBN:    0-9650275-1-1
Library of Congress Catalog Card Number: 96-78878

Published in the United States of America by the Loving Heart Holistic Health Center, Post Office Box 1829, Carrollton, Georgia, 30117-7129, U.S.A

Printed in the U.S.A.        1st Edition 1997

This book was printed by Darby Printing Company (6215 Purdue Drive, Atlanta, Georgia, 30336, U.S.A.). In order to encourage a healthy environment, Darby Printing Company recycles the following items: waste paper; cardboard rollstock cores; film; silver; Eco Systems developer (used for plate processing); Web plates; as well as Sheetfed plates, waste ink, oil, and blanket wash. Additionally, ink totes are used for their Web Press (resulting in no waste ink); partially recycled paper is used in their Web Press, and soy-based ink is primarily used for all of their printing.

**THIS BOOK HAS BEEN PRINTED ON PARTIALLY RECYCLED, ACID-FREE PAPER, WITH ENVIRONMENTALLY FRIENDLY SOY-BASED INK.**

# CATCH the VISION, Find Your MISSION

## How to Master Your True Destiny.

## A Treasure of Golden Wisdom.

**Published in the U.S.A. by
The Loving Heart Holistic Health Center.**

## About the Author

Andrew Nelson is presently the CEO of a multi-media computer company. Additionally, he writes and conducts workshops that integrate spirituality into various topics dealing with personal development.

Andrew presently lives in England, but travels extensively around the world. He enjoys helping people to reach their higher potentials, and discover the infinity of their true selves. Andrew has many interests, including Tai chi, holistic health, mountain climbing, walking in the wilderness, and adventure.

## Acknowledgements

I would like to especially acknowledge the following people. I have learned so much in so many ways through their love, understanding and perception of life. For reasons of anonymity some people have been left off this list. *(Names listed alphabetically)*

Mom and Dad
Greg Kuschwara
Ron Mitchell
Katrina Nalenza
Rosemary Palmerton
Richard Patton
Mike Pelham
Jon Richings

## Introduction

This book is for anyone who wants to master their destiny in this life, for those who want to have and live the brightest, most inspiring dream possible, by discovering their true purpose.

Maybe you are at a crossroads or turning point in life. You don't know which way to go next or how to take the next step. This book will certainly help you to understand the purpose of these junctions in life, and how to move ahead.

Perhaps your life is in a rut and you cannot move forward or see how to improve your situation. If you are tired of the same old patterns and situations reoccurring in your life, this book will help you to replace the old patterns with a Soul inspired adventure that comes from the heart.

Life is filled with lessons and it is up to us whether we keep on retaking the same old lessons or move on. We can change our life for the better irrespective of age or circumstance.

Take this step to find your mission in life, and in doing so all of life around you will improve beyond measure. So come and join me in the journey of your lifetime!

# A Personal Dedication

I dedicate this book to You.
To your every success in life,
To understanding your true nature,
To unlocking the genius within you,
To being the very best you can possibly become,

To catching Soul's vision,
To turning the vision into a mission,
To following through on your mission.

Soul has gently guided you thus far,
And Soul waits patiently.
The doorway to higher truths is open,
Your path is before you,
Your destiny awaits.

# Table of Contents

## Tools for the Journey

You will require two sets of index or address cards, available from most stationery stores. I suggest that you select a set of yellow cards, and a bold marker pen.

There are also some basic things that I would invite you to start practicing everyday. It is very important to build up a personal rhythm that works for you. This makes things easier to do rather than a burden, similar to washing the dishes. It is a burden if you seldom wash up, but when done regularly, there is little struggle.

### Somewhere to Contemplate

There are a number of people who have practiced meditation, but I would like to introduce you to the concept of contemplation. It is a quiet time with your true self, Soul. A time where you can, through special spiritual exercises, tune into your Soul state.

Simply put we are first Soul. The moment we accept this, our lower consciousness begins to release the tight grip over our life, and we become more Soul centered. Things begin to flow more in our life. So by accepting that we are first Soul, meditation becomes contemplation which is then centered in divine love. I am mentioning this now as you will need to find somewhere in your home where you can comfortably contemplate everyday, without being disturbed.

It is important to put aside a time everyday for personal study. I prefer the early hours of the morning as the silence and stillness of the world allows me to become aware of myself as Soul. This stillness allows me to create a path that I can follow through the day. By setting aside a time when you can study and create your future for that day, week, month, or lifetime you will set up an unstoppable rhythm. It will gather momentum every time you put energy into it. Eventually it will become a rolling wave, whose crest you will ride until you reach your destiny.

## Working with your Partner

If you are in a loving relationship it is perfectly fine to work on the contemplations (spiritual exercises) together. That means instead of memorizing and doing them solo, you ask your partner to read the spiritual exercises out to you. If this is done slowly and with love while you close your eyes, you will become absorbed in the spiritual journey. Some people record the spiritual exercises on tape and play them back which achieves the same effect. You need to find what works for you. It is just as effective to work solo as it is with a partner. The only difference is preference.

## Your Mission Journal

I would like to invite you to maintain a Mission Journal, and if possible write out a label and place it on the cover. I suggest a label similar to the one that follows.

---

# Mission Journal
# My Special Mission in Life

Name:

Start Date:

---

As far as the journal goes, all you need is a large blank letter size journal or a diary. If you choose a diary pick one that has one page per day. An example of an entry might be:

| Sunday 1st January | Monday 2nd January |
|---|---|
| *Dreams last night* | *Dreams last night* |
| *Goals for Today* | *Goals for Today* |
| *What have I learned/observed* | *What have I learned/observed* |

I would also encourage you to obtain a small notepad so that you can jot down notes and ideas you have during the day. This is much easier than trying to remember them until you can write them down later in your Mission Journal. Sometimes when ideas come they are like ladders into a higher state of consciousness. We need to climb these ladders, and the best way is to write down what flows through our mind. This connects the inner experience to our outer physical world.

## <u>Your Dedication</u>

At this point it is important to make a dedication to yourself about discovering your mission in life. I have written some words that may work for you, or if you prefer you may like to choose your own.

I am Soul,
therefore I am dedicated to my
mission in life.
I acknowledge this greatness within.

It is from Soul,
from this true greatness
that I see my mission in life.
I accept each step I take as part of my unfolding mission.

I will use what I can in this book,
together with all of the gifts in life,
to find my mission,
to master my destiny.

Today is a new day in my unique journey
to discover my special mission.
My expectations are limitless.

Your Name

Signature

Date

# Your Personal Workshop

## Making It Work for You!

Simplicity is the main aim here. It is said that the greatest truth is always expressed in the greatest simplicity, so I have tried to make the explanations and exercises as simple as possible. To get the best from this book I suggest the following study pattern.

1. Read the book through once without skipping any sections, but don't do any of the exercises.

2. Wait at least <u>three days</u>.

3. Now read Chapter One, making notes and doing the exercises. Allow <u>one week</u> for this phase.

4. Now read Chapter Two and spend <u>four weeks</u> doing these exercises unless you truly feel you have mastered this topic.

5. Next read Chapter Three. Spend <u>one week</u> on these exercises.

6. This should be sufficient to prepare you for the first main aspect of this book within Chapter Four, Catching the Vision.

I am reminded of two things here. First, an old song "Take Time to Be Holy." Second, an old Irish saying "The one thing God gave in abundance when the earth was created was time." If you force spiritual unfoldment to happen you will lose it, followed in short order by your patience.

# Let Me Introduce Myself

*I was born in 1961 on Sunday, October 22nd at 12 o'clock midday. Outside the weather was still warm but the leaves were starting to fall from turning yellow, like a last burst of sunshine before the bleak winter.*

*As devout Christians, my parents schooled me from a young age in the ways of Christianity, but from these early beginnings I knew that I had a mission in life that was outside of my parents' religion. I seemed to be able to touch on wisdom way beyond my undeveloped mind. As Soul I was able to travel into higher states of awareness beyond the physical, into realms so beautiful, so filled with divine love that this world seemed dark and claustrophobic upon my return.*

*Children often travel as Soul naturally into the heavenly worlds, but most lose this art as they grow up, especially when told to stop daydreaming by adults.*

*By the time I was eighteen, my search for divine love, wisdom and truth had taken me into Kung Fu. Here I studied a Northern style called Juen Yen Kuen Fa. This was a very hard traditional style of martial art. The philosophy was simply this, "Push yourself beyond exhaustion and you will begin to draw on your inner resources of Chi." (Chinese for the body's life force). This, coupled with special meditation techniques developed the flow of Chi. After a few years, it began to work with very startling results. It marked a milestone in my life. But still my hunger for divine truth was not satisfied. So I decided to study some of the Eastern religions and many of the psychic arts to see if they would lead me to truth, but still I was no closer. I seemed* to be exchanging bits of the jigsaw puzzle, yet never seeing the whole picture. Then one night while in a dream I became conscious, and as Soul I soared out of the dream. Beside me was a very wise spiritual teacher of Chinese origin. I asked him to help me discover my purpose in life. It took less than a few days for my life to begin to shape up. Everything began to fall into place. It was as if I had gotten off the rocky footpath and onto the main road.

From then on, I began to see all people as individual divine Souls. I began to understand that we were not born as peasants, but as true heroes. That our lives, if we chose, could be filled with abundance rather than poverty of thought, action or life. Writing this book became part of my journey. A simple way of helping you, should you also wish to discover this greatness, this abundance, this divine love, and your very own unique purpose in life. I truly hope this book will help all those who know that there is something more to life than the cradle to grave existence, who feel that they have something to contribute to life, but can never quite put a finger on what it is.

## Spiritual Foundations

The foundations for this book were established after an early mid life crisis at the age of 27. The business I had always dreamed of began to crash. It was a long, slow and painful death. It was like jumping off a high board, knowing that there was only concrete below, and to make it worse, it seemed to occur in slow motion. I guess I proved the old statement that says, "If a challenge in life does not destroy you, it will only serve to make you stronger." Well, out of the ashes I came across a man, who was like a spiritual master. He seemed so filled with *divine energy, to the point that whenever I met him for a chat, things suddenly worked out in my life. At the time I did not know how or why, I was just grateful for the experience. I later discovered that it was the light within his being that served to re-ignite and thus illuminate my consciousness. That from this illuminated state all problems could be solved in a fraction of the time usually required. We would have many conversations a day on the telephone and they would go on for hours.*

*He was the only person that seemed able to fulfill my eternal thirst of knowledge and wisdom, not once but several times a day. Throughout all of this, he helped me to understand that I was first Soul. That I had much more to give than I had already given in life, and that my mission in life had only just begun. Out of the ashes of my life I was to arise, and become more than I ever was before.*

*It was hard at first to change my focus away from my problems and failures. I was like the person who continually focused on the death of the caterpillar rather than on the birth of a beautiful butterfly, but my ignorance was short lived. I practiced a number of spiritual exercises that enabled me to tune into my true self, and I began to see my mission in life unfold before me like a beautiful tapestry. My mission in life was also re-confirmed in a dream where I found myself in a sacred golden temple situated in a beautiful spiritual dimension of existence. This place seemed so familiar. I knew I had been here many times in the dream state. I walked through the temple gates, and into a sanctuary area where I was warmly greeted by what I can only describe as an infinitely divine being. As I looked at this being I recognized him. He had been with me guiding my life for a long time. He was my guardian angel. With this* realization my heart simply overflowed with love and gratitude. We talked and he explained that I had a mission in life, something more than my common duties and responsibilities. He illuminated in front of me a picture of my future, my mission in life.

I remembered some of the dream when I awoke. I decided that I really had to put my life back together again, find my mission, discover my destiny, and master it.

I learned a lot in the next five years, and I decided to put my experiences down in a book to help other seekers. The harsh experiences in my life challenged and changed my life completely. From being a beggar at the mercy of every whim and wave of change in life, I slowly began to understand each change and ride each wave. For once I could appreciate what it must be like to be a master yachtsman, riding each wave on the high seas while still enjoying the journey.

I was later to catch Soul's vision of my mission in life, and I can only describe it as a most beautiful shock. It was much like discovering someone who you had truly loved as a child, yet had later lost touch with, was in fact still alive and living just a few blocks away.

When I recognized my mission, an inner wind began to gently flow through my life, and I gracefully began to sail in a new direction that was exciting and challenging. At every twist and turn and bump I was alive with excitement. I could not wait for the next day to arrive with its challenges and blessings. As I met each challenge I experienced a blessing, so I sailed a little higher and wiser than before. Step by step I began to live the life I had dreamed as Soul, all those many years ago. My whole perspective on life changed by the moment and for *the better. I became as a baby Eagle soaring ever nearer the mountain top on a mid summer's day. The winds were strong. It was sometimes hard to stay on course, but the winds made me stronger, and the deepest joy was the knowledge that this was only the beginning of a fantastic journey.*

*I have presented all the techniques, and methods in this book at a number of workshops, discussion groups and talks. All I can say is that it is a joy to watch people's lives change for the better. However, I must mention that a method or technique of itself will not change anything in your life for you need to take action. All this book does is help you find your own spiritual gateways. You must walk through your own gateways to find your destiny. So I encourage you to expect results, expect the best simply because you deserve it. Not everything in life adds up like two plus two to make four. Sometimes you have to go higher, to Soul, your true heart center.*

**Follow your dreams into the heart of Soul and your life will begin to flow with an unequalled joy. It is your destiny should you choose it.**

# Chapter 1.
# What Is a Mission?

## Understanding What a Mission in Life Is, and How Our True Nature Shapes Our Experiences.

As Soul we are amazing, beautiful, boundless and beyond compare. We share the highest qualities of God which are divine love, wisdom, knowledge, spiritual power and freedom. The question is, how much of this vast spiritual heritage do we use in our daily life? Is our perception of life great or small? Do we see greatness in everyone we meet? And do we daily experience the blessings of life? We simply did not come into existence the moment we were born. As Soul we chose to be here for a very special reason.

Soul, the infinite part of you, chose this lifetime with all of its restrictions, politics, religions, environments, problems, difficulties, pleasures and possibilities. It was chosen because it was a great challenge. It would serve as the furnace that melts the finest gold from the rock, and this gold is the greatness in Soul, the real YOU.

This world is a tough place and the lessons sometimes hard. So often in the midst of the difficulty the mind panics. It wrestles control of a situation away from Soul which is always gently guiding with love, kindness and wisdom through the stormy seas of life.

We are Soul, and only from the high viewpoint of Soul can the stormy seas of life be mastered. We each came here with a specific mission. Our mission is our greatest challenge. We can also have many missions in life depending on our purpose. In accepting our mission in life we get all the help we can accept from the divine source of all life. Our mission is a unique journey into destiny. Each day as we progress we unwrap the dull coats that have hidden our true colors and our true splendor. As this happens we will begin to see the magnificent greatness of Soul unfold in our understanding, thoughts, actions and situations.

If you were to ask yourself where you are going in life, would you be able to give yourself a straight answer, or would you "um", and "er" about it? If you don't know where you are going in life you will most certainly end up somewhere else, simply because you are not mastering your life.

There is no point in denying ourselves the fabulous spiritual wealth we have as Soul. Within this spiritual wealth are the seeds for the mission or missions we have in life. As the pace of life quickens, and nations rise and fall, it becomes imperative that each person accept the challenge of their mission in life so that they may excel in mastering life and destiny. **It is time for each person who is awake to the call of Soul to turn on the lights and come out from under the trees, and shine the light of Soul into their lives. To live the brightest, most inspiring dream possible, the dream of a lifetime. - A mission second to none, fit only for a true hero. This is what awaits us should we choose to find and follow through on our mission in life.**

## A Golden Key

There are no bounds to what our mission in life can be. It could be with business, family, personal, financial, health, research, inventions, the list is endless. However, the main distinguishing feature of a mission is that whatever it is that you do, it makes a difference for the better for more than just yourself. Simply put, **YOU LOOK FOR LOVE IN EVERY ACTIVITY. YOU ENTER THE ACTIVITY WITH LOVE AND YOU LEAVE THE ACTIVITY GLOWING WITH YOUR LOVE.** A mission always serves life for the best. Many people are unconscious that they are fulfilling their mission in life while others know what their purpose in life is, and carry out their mission. Living your mission in life does not necessarily mean that you will be well known and famous like some, but you will be happy living an effective life, fulfilled beyond measure.

## We Have Both a Duty and a Mission in Life

One of the most important things we can learn is how to expand our consciousness beyond the everyday hum drum of life, and into the higher states of consciousness. This is where we can find our true identity, and our real mission in life as Soul. It is from these exhalted states of consciousness that we will discover the true greatness within ourselves, to become the infinite fountain of divine love and wisdom that burns brightly in the loving heart of Soul. Every Soul has both a DUTY in life, and a MISSION in life. The duty is usually what we do every day of our life to survive, or to support our family. For most people, <u>without the balance of a mission in their life</u>, the duty becomes a very repetitious chore, a heavy burden that entails worry, concern, heartache and emotional stress. Obviously, it is not like this all the time as everything moves in cycles.

There is a simple way for us, as Soul, to once again take control of our lives. If we observe life, we will see that so many people start out with a great script on life all about the successes and experiences they want. However, all too soon everyone else begins to add to this script. After a short while, this person has lost the plot. Unknowingly they become an actor in other people's scripts. A slave to the whims and wishes of others. In fact the whole journey becomes so muddled that people can become enslaved without even realizing it.

In the Western world we talk about our great lands of freedom, yet how many people truly have freedom? Do you have the freedom to do what you like, when you like, and how you like or to freely follow any creative pursuit you wish? Ask yourself how much of your life is governed by duties and how much comes from freedom, the freedom to BE.

We live in a world increasingly governed by technology and the people who drive this technology both politically and technically. Technology in its highest expression is our servant. It gives us more time to spend with our loved ones and do other things we love to do. Sadly, the opposite is far too often true. Every day millions of people are forced to work harder, for less employment security and in many cases, less pay. At the heart of this is a drive to make the production cost of merchandise and products ever cheaper so profits will be higher. Now contrary to what a lot of people think, businesses are set up by their owners for their owners and share holders. This is why the employees seldom benefit with more free time and money. This tends to be the reserve of the owners and share holders only.

Increasingly people are becoming slaves to the speed that technology is driving their lives. There is precious little time left in a day for creative and Soul expressive pursuits, for these are the things that bring spiritual freedom.

People used to work from 9am to 5pm, but now it is more likely to be from 8am to 6pm or longer. If technology was being correctly applied we would be working from 9am to 3pm. There are many who love the speed and buzz that a fast technology driven life gives them, but this may be an illusion of true success and freedom. In these situations we need to be careful how much of our individuality and personal power we surrender to outside control. Maybe we need to ask ourself the question, "Can I walk away from these situations and still remain in balance, or would my life collapse." The human spirit is controlled when it is trapped in illusions unable to have the freedom to BE itself. Freedom is absolutely important if we are to realize and pursue our highest purposes in life.

The more people pursue money as a destiny in itself the less control they will have over their lives. However, abundance is a quality of Soul and when we express abundance, money can become a by-product. This way no matter how wealthy we become no one can take it away. We become like the person with the Midas touch. Everything we do turns to success because it comes from within. We no longer have to be worried when stocks and shares crash on the markets, as money is just one effect of how we may have chosen to express our abundance. The same inner raw material and energy used to create the wealth in the first place can be used time and time again. This is living life from Soul, from the state of causation and not effect. **Our true greatness, our true destiny begins to unfold like a fresh spring rose on a sunny day the moment we allow Soul to run our life**.

If our mind is our master then we can be controlled by the arguments and persuasion of others. This occurs because we have blocked the gentle guidance of Soul from flowing into our life. However, if Soul is truly in control nothing can control us. Soul radiates love, and the first quality of love is freedom. So with Soul in control, we can experience greater love and greater freedom.

One thing about life is that the harder it gets the less some of us rely on our higher instincts, and the more we become part of the problem. We just make the problem bigger. For example...

*Imagine two people driving to work. Both leave late. The first driver, Bob, is desperate. Afraid of being late he drives as fast as he can. He thinks that the traffic is going extra slow today just because he is late. He is tense and aggressive, shouting abusively at anyone who looks mildly like a hindrance to him. Mary, the other driver, leaves for work just as late, but she takes it easy. Having left late Mary accepts she is in a later time frame, and so she relaxes, notices the birds and the deer by the roadside. Because she is relaxed she has not restricted the flow of divine love. This beautiful life-giving force flows through her life keeping her in tune with Soul. As she drives along she gets a nudge from Soul to turn left and go a new way. Unknowingly she avoids an accident up ahead that Bob is about to get held up in, simply because he is too tense to tune into Soul, and is working against life by pushing and barging his way to work.*

When life gets tough our state of awareness can begin to drop from the high regions of Soul. Bob's anger had dropped his consciousness to the point where he felt that he was his car. If anyone came within a foot of his car he would shout at them. The more he perceived himself as the car the worse life became for him as he felt closed in. But it was just a perception. He identified with the lowest thing possible rather than the highest, which is Soul. He was no more the car before the journey than he was after the journey. On the other hand Mary was so relaxed that she would not have cared if other cars were too close, for she knew that she was Soul. She was much greater than the situation.

This is why life is our greatest teacher. It lovingly shows us step by step how to live life from Soul, from our loving center. This world is a big school with many rooms. Our teachers have been many, including Plato, Churchill,

Socrates, Shakespeare, Einstein, Beethoven, Martin Luther King, Jesus, Mohammed, and many more. All have come to give us special lessons in life. Obviously, just like in school, some dislike what is being said while some will grasp the higher viewpoint from which the words are spoken.

In everyday life there is so much pressure to succeed, to equal the next person, to bring home enough money to pay bills, to buy this product or go to that place. This inevitably leads to most people becoming enslaved to artificial problems and self made illusions, to the point that most forget that they have more than just a duty in life. Embarking on our mission makes us more individualized. This makes us less susceptible to the subtle process of conforming to other people's goals and ambitions. The subtle pressures to conform come from peer groups, from the media, and from what governments want you to do or think. These are all wrapped up in the duties we do. Soon the inner dream, the mission we as Soul have, begins to fall asleep. I recall this short story about conforming...

*When I was a child I used to go to church every Sunday, without fail. I had no choice in the matter. This church was a very strict church called the Brethren. It was extremely sombre, not a smile or a hint of humor. So I believed that holiness or spirituality was being very severe and sombre. I kept on hearing about the wrath of God, but somehow this did not tally with my inner knowledge of this divine source which simply radiated love no matter what I did. This divine source that I knew never judged anyone.*

*The thing that I really hated about church was having to wear my "Sunday best", which at that time was a suit with* short trousers. I always thought that whoever invented short trousers for small boys must have done so in the knowledge that it made their legs easier to be smacked.

Anyway, one Sunday morning my brother and I decided that we wanted to conform to the breaking of the bread, and drinking of the wine, which was done every Sunday by the church elders. I was just four years old then, and my brother was seven, but we had never taken the wine or bread, and it was bugging us. As children we felt the need to conform to be the same as adults. So we plotted our scheme as small boys do. We took some bread, some red grape juice, and two glasses with us to church, all hidden in our jackets.

The meeting was sombre and serious as usual, and everyone was deeply into silence which for a young boy was hard. It was not five minutes, it was an hour of silence punctuated by three or four songs that had no musical accompaniment, and long prayers that seemed to never end, then silence again. Well, they got to the breaking of the bread and sharing of the wine, which symbolized Christ and the Crucifixion. So my brother and I saw our chance to be involved and grown up. We gave each other a lump of bread and poured out our "red wine" into the glasses and drank. We then pretended to go into a deep holy state, which lasted for all of fifteen seconds! The looks and thoughts of disgust pouring across the room put an end to our holy state, but I did feel good inside. I felt that I was one of them even if they did not want me to be in their group.

After the service this stunt was looked upon gravely by some. Others saw the funny side, saying, "boys will be boys." To me it was more like "boys want to be men."

*Several years later I met friends who went to a charismatic church. This is one where they jump for joy, talk in tongues (a biblical spiritual language) and openly praise Jesus. The first time I went, I was startled by this behavior of jumping, clapping and talking in a strange language. But my friend told me that it was praising God, so I soon conformed. There I was, a few weeks later jumping in the air, clapping my hands and praising Jesus. Then I asked myself, "Is this me or is this what my friends want me to be? Where is my individuality in all this?" so I stopped going to church, for it was not me.*

This is how conforming sometimes starts. You do something different and you get several other people who want to do it also. There is a phrase used nowadays "Why don't you get a life?" Although it is cynical, there is a lot of truth in it. We actually need to **GET OUR OWN LIFE BACK**. Conforming can start out by one person arguing that you must do this thing, because it is great. Then two convince two more, and those four convince four more. Eventually you have a section of the nation all doing the same thing.

It is like brand advertising in sportswear which creates the myth, "If you are serious you will wear a particular brand of sports gear." Like lemmings many go out and buy that brand. All of this has to do with the fear of BEING an individual, because it is far easier to be a lemming.

If we conform to the desires and goals of others we can forget that we too have a special mission in life, a mission that only we can perform. A mission that can transform and expand the consciousness and understanding of life from common knowledge into divine wisdom and knowledge. **Having a mission will allow us to move**

**through life with a true sense of purpose flowing within our own spiritual current.** We become a cause moving in a specific spiritual direction. This way life becomes crafted with divine love and filled with wisdom. We no longer drift where the tides of life take us, but become the creator of a life filled with adventure, love, wisdom, personal effectiveness and creative power.

Our life here is a gift and in its true sense we will only discover the contents of the gift when we unwrap it and look inside. Too often our talents in life stay on the top shelf gathering dust. Usually this is because the last time we unwrapped it and looked inside, it did not work out the way we expected. We wanted a particular goal in life and it did not happen at the precise moment we wanted it. Or we wanted the pain to stop and it continued despite our prayers. Or the struggle to make our life any different was just too great. The comfort zone we created was too deep to escape. Maybe we lost our sense of direction in life and every different thing we tried seemed to be just like a band aid, never really healing the deep wound of dissatisfaction.

Eventually, we wrapped up our talents in their beautiful paper, put the package back on the top shelf and returned to admiring it from a distance. We need to unwrap this gift of life, re-discover what it can offer, and in a courageous way work with the tools we have. Soon we will begin to tap into the unlimited abundance of love, wisdom, knowledge and power that is our inheritance.

When I look at life I see it as a divine stream of blessings that tries to help and nurture the individual spirit in every way so we can become the true master of life. Many with strong minds think that they are the master, but they are merely the slave who has managed to quell the inner rebellion. I say this because the mind is a poor master, as it has not the subtlety to work with the various energies that our emotions require. Neither are our emotions suitable masters for our life.

## Surrendering to Soul

The only way we can truly live life in a balanced way is to surrender control of our life to Soul. From this higher level of consciousness, life will begin to flow.

The mind can take us down difficult, logical alleyways of left or right, good or bad. There are no in betweens. The mind tends to bark out orders like an Army Colonel to make us do something. We have probably had the experience where we find ourselves saying, "I've got to do it. I've got to do it. Come on do it." Yet if we listen to ourselves it sounds so aggressive, and kind of "do it or you die." Where is the love?

This is an example of the mind losing control of events and resorting to the primitive raw energy.

It may appear to work for some, but the result is that it damages the emotional self and can cause damage to our vital energy centers which ultimately leads to ill health.

Soul never takes on something it cannot do, and it finds smart ways to solve problems. This same scenario run again from Soul's viewpoint would be the soft knowing voice within your heart that says, "I can do it." Then love wells up in your heart, or Soul begins to move in a particular direction by pushing the energy out there first. If the emotions or mind feel uncomfortable, it withdraws and Soul reassesses the situation. It knows that success is a matter of viewpoint, so it changes the viewpoint and tries again. We normally experience this as pondering at a possible choice because it does not feel quite right. We wait and wonder what other solutions are possible. This is the action of Soul. Sooner or later an attitude and direction fit the physical body, the emotions and the mind. We then take action and succeed. There is no barking of orders. Moving through life like this is simply beautiful. There is no stress, no worry, just love and warmth towards life.

## What is Consciousness?

This brings me onto consciousness. From Soul's viewpoint, consciousness is the degree to which you are aware of your entire being. Our entire being effectively consists of six specific states of consciousness. Each state of consciousness is a more refined reflection of the human self. Consider this. When you sleep at night there is a part of you that continues to function. It exists in a world that is usually brighter and more perceptive than this physical world. For most people, this is their emotional self. But it can be a much higher state, even Soul.

When you wake up in the morning, your inner vessels (Soul body, mind body, etc.) do not got to sleep. You continue to experience your emotions during the day. You can take a quick nap and have an entire dream experience in a matter of seconds. It is only your physical self that needs to sleep. The two ways we experience our emotional self is during the day when we experience emotions, and during sleep when we can have dreams. These dreams are as real as in the physical world and in most cases even more real and dynamic.

What I am saying is that we have an emotional self, that functions independently of the physical self, but forms part of our total consciousness through which we experience life. It is a much more refined body in comparison to the physical in terms of vibration. That is why the physical eyes cannot see it. It exists on what is called the Astral Plane. Consider for a moment, temperature. It exists on a level beyond the perception of the eyes. So all we can do is feel it and see the effects of it. This is just like the emotions. We can feel them and see the effects of emotive behavior.

Now, apart from the emotional self, we have three more finer vessels through which we as Soul can consciously experience life. These are the Causal, Mental, Etheric, and finally the pure essence, Soul. I use the term vessel because Soul is the source. It fills each vessel with this life force, yet the vessels are but a reflection of Soul, a means for Soul to gain experience in these coarse lower worlds. All of these vessels occupy the same space and effective time, and if you could see auras in people you would see these vessels as being slightly larger than the physical body and of varying colors.

When you sleep at night the other people you perceive in your dreams are either on the Astral Plane, or the Mental Plane, or maybe even on the Soul Plane and above. These are real spiritual experiences you are having every night.

## Spiritual Energy Centers

Each of Soul's outer garments, or lower selves, or vessels are connected to the physical body via the chakras. These are energy centers in the body. Energy flows between all the bodies via these chakras. Many people experience things like a lump in the throat when they have been humiliated. This is the ego, which is a part of the mental self, flowing with unbalanced energy, and we feel it in the throat chakra. Sometimes we feel butterflies in the abdomen when we have to do something that is making us nervous like taking an exam. This is the emotional self out of balance flowing unbalanced energy through the emotional chakra. Or how about shivers down the back of the spine or over our head, or maybe an expansiveness around the head? This is Soul communicating with us in its usual loving way. The spiritual energy of Soul flows through the crown chakra located at the top of our head.

When Soul is in control: | When the mind is in control:

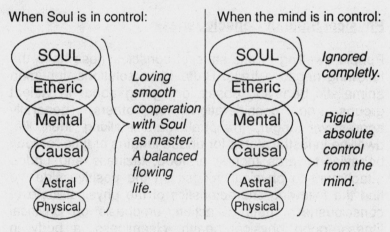

To master our mission in life we need to keep all our vessels, or centers of consciousness, balanced. This means allowing Soul to be the master and all of the other vessels equal servants co-operating to produce effective actions. This naturally begins to occur as we progress with our mission and begin to use the spiritual exercises.

The chakras are the heart centers for each vessel. They pump the vital life force around each vessel, just as the heart pumps blood around the physical vessel. Each of our inner bodies, or vessels are linked together by a stream of energy from Soul, and although each inner vessel exists in its own dimension they are all merged so totally and completely that most people never experience any separateness. We need all of these vessels to function in this physical world. So let's take a closer look at them, and the characteristics of our consciousness as it shifts between them. This should allow a better understanding of the the source of our thoughts, feelings and actions.

## Physical State of Consciousness

People dwelling in this state of consciousness have the following negative traits: Brute force solutions, inhuman animalistic behavior, obsession, going about in violent groups, no consideration for others, generally aggressive, anger, irrational fears stalking their life, dwelling in lustful states for undue lengths of time, greedy behavior towards money or food, laziness and undue attachment to physical things. On the positive side we find the following characteristics of the physical state of consciousness: Lots of action, emphasis on physical fitness, good physical health, cleanliness, a body in complete control, a relaxed body at ease with itself, physical beauty and a very responsive body.

## Emotional State of Consciousness

The Astral body deals with all of our emotional needs. The Astral Plane where it resides, is a vast region that is similar to the physical universe, but brighter, kinder, and much more loving and creative. This is also where many people have their dreams at night, simply because the emotional self, through stress etc., can become unbalanced during the day and needs its energy to be re-balanced.

Looking at the emotional self we find on the negative side of this state of consciousness: Lots of whims, spurts of energy, inability to concentrate for long periods of time, swings of feelings about aspects of your life, depression, instability, moodiness, inability to carry out plans, lots of talk and no action, laying guilt trips on others, feeling guilty, emotive anger and wrath. On the positive side of the emotional level we find the following: A steady emotive focus, a balanced flow of energy through the day, balanced feelings, emotional happiness, musical talents, creative expression, a good ability at acting, joking, very friendly attitudes, sympathy, sensing something is right or wrong without really having hard facts, overwhelmingly good feelings and great enthusiasm.

## Causal State of Consciousness

This is where our memory resides and the log of events past and present. The Causal region is also the place from which people are able to see into the future of events that are to come. However, it must be noted that this is a limited capability. All you can do from the Causal region is see possibilities based on current circumstances. Anyone with good common sense and the right information could do a similar job. Only from the Soul state of consciousness can you see the true and exact future that lies in front of you. The Casual level is reached by many who meditate, through chanting words such as AUM. Looking at the traits of this state of consciousness we find on the negative side someone who is constantly looking back into the past, who is nostalgic, who has an inability to deal with today, who thinks that the past is better than the present, who is always talking about the past, or who lives in the future, who lives with fantasies about how they will be one day, but never does anything about it. This state is also the source of a poor memory. On the positive side, if you harness the power from this state of consciousness then you will be the sort of person who has their feet firmly planted in the here and now. You know where you are going and never dwell too long in the past. You also have a good memory.

## Mental State of Consciousness

The Mental region is a magnificent world tinged with blue light. It is truly an incredible place, almost beyond description. This is the region where reason and intellect, or logical thinking originates. This is the home of philosophy and you will find many philosophies at various stages of development in the many wisdom schools in this region. Those who have mental issues to resolve have their dreams here and they find quick answers. However, if they worry about the problem then it sinks them back to the emotional level where there are no answers to the intellectual problems. The Mental dimension or world is where language originates. We can find many new languages here for all of the billions of different universes that exist below the Soul Plane. The Mental state is a very dominant state of consciousness. It makes a great servant to Soul, but a poor master of life. The negative side of this state of consciousness is: Panic attacks, rigid rules in your life, inability to change your viewpoint, inability to see other viewpoints, bigotry, erratic behaviors, extreme views, extreme actions, inability to see subtle points, or to be subtle, and also insensitivity.

On the positive side we find such fine points as: Strong character and personality, agile thinking, good at mathematics and problem solving, determination, good concentration, quick thinking and decisiveness.

## Etheric State of Consciousness

This is a very charged region of great light tinged with a majestic purple. It is where all of our intuition resides. The Etheric body works here to keep all of our automatic functions working and in order, like breathing, healing wounds, control of how cells age, etc. It is the gateway to Soul. Psychologists call this the subconscious state, but in reality it is the super conscious as it keeps us alive. It does not really have a negative state worth mentioning as it is so close to the Soul consciousness.

## Soul State of Consciounsess

The last and highest state of consciousness is Soul centered. This is the real you. This state of consciousness has no limits, is infinite, and can best be described by qualities like divine love, wisdom, knowledge, spiritual power, joy, happiness, courage, vision, abundance, infinity, greatness, adventuresome, spiritual strength, adaptability, flexibility, an infinite viewpoint and a spiritual character. This Soul centered state is the ideal way to live our lives. Anything less makes us less than who we truly are. To master our mission we need to be the master of our consciousness, which means being Soul centered most of the time. That way our lower bodies can co-operate with each other under the guidance of Soul. This simple action makes us effective in life.

In the Soul Plane regions of endless light, where Soul resides, there is no duality like positive and negative, good and bad, night and day, rich and poor, or anger and peace. Everything in the Soul Plane and beyond is infinite, abundant, vast and beautiful. Everything here begins with love and never ends. These worlds are bathed with the most incredible melody, which comes from the light. This is the light and sound of God or put another way, this is divine love. Here we find the true origin of nature and life itself in all the worlds below. Plants here are huge and radiate the most majestic light. In fact everything here has its purest expression.

## Endless Regions of Light

As much as Soul expands in consciousness it can never become God, only more God-like. I am only a beginner, and have only just begun to explore these regions. They are endless worlds upon worlds, each one brighter, and I mean a billion, billion, billion times brighter than the light on Earth. That is why only Soul can exist in these regions above the Etheric worlds. Once you have been to these regions consciously or unconsciously it is impossible to return to this Physical world with the same attitude as before. You will be filled with so much love you will be a light unto this world. You will find yourself affecting other people's lives just by being in their presence. This is because the flow of divine love serves all unconditionally. Many people travel to these high inner worlds like the Soul Plane or above, during sleep. Upon awakening they have true joy in their hearts, or they feel truly inspired and know not why. Sometimes they say, "What a wonderful day!", and people wonder, what it is that makes them so happy, especially when it is cold and wet outside. It is as if nothing can upset them or ever go wrong during their day. They shine with love all day long.

Some people have a misconception about heaven. They think that heaven is a one stop perfect place where angels wait on their every need and people float about on fluffy white clouds. This view is far from the truth. Earth, in this physical universe, is a level of heaven, albeit a very low one. There are many, in fact infinite levels in heaven, and in each one there is work to be done. Even when we reach the Soul Plane, which is the first of the pure worlds, there is work to be done.

When I talk about reaching these levels, it is more a case of being able to shift one's consciousness (attention) from where it is, to a finer level. Much like changing your attitude. Instead of seeing weeds we see wildflowers and silver blue dragon flies, and so on.

Creation in the lower worlds follow set lines. However, when we reach the Soul Plane and beyond, we enter into infinity and freedom. Creation from here onwards has unknown boundaries. We are the creator, the composer, the orchestra and the instruments. Here the imagination is solid. That means whatever we imagine is exactly what we get, and we get it immediately. As there is no negativity, everything created is beautiful and inspiring.

Souls who are conscious at this level seldom if ever abuse this gift of creativity, for they have already evolved through the lower states of the emotions and mind stuff. However, the kingdom of heaven has to be won everyday. There is no sitting back with feet up expecting it to be plain sailing from here on in. Every step along the way has to be earned with love and courage.

## Soul Realization and God Realization

Soul Realization is the degree to which you are aware of yourself as Soul. This realization occurs in degrees. Everything that has life has a degree of this Soul Realization. The more you can engage yourself in life from the heart of Soul, the greater the awareness of your true infinity becomes. You begin to experience the boundless qualities of Soul; love, wisdom, power, creativity and joy. These are just a few of the infinite qualities of Soul that begin to pour through your being as you move into deeper states of Soul Realization. However, these magnificent qualities need an outer expression to anchor them. They are like beautiful flowers, unless they have earth and water they will wither and die. Your mission in life is the earth and water through which Soul will truly flourish. As you move into deeper states of Soul Realization, so too do you move into deeper states of God Realization. There are no boundaries, however, at some point, you become so filled with this light and sound, this unconditional divine love, that you become more God-like. Many people experience glimpses of these higher states of consciousness. However, the purpose of life is to learn how to maintain and unfold these higher states of consciousness while leading a balanced life.

## Engaging Soul More Fully in Our Life

The key to engaging Soul more fully in our life begins when we ask ourselves questions like, "Is there more to life?" or "Do I have a purpose in life?" or "What is my mission in life?" **THE VISION OF YOUR MISSION IS BORN IN THE PURE HIGHER SOUL WORLDS.**

I would like to conclude this first chapter with a simple spiritual exercise which will build and strengthen the light, this divine love, within you.

## Spiritual Exercise

*Find a place in your home where you will not be disturbed for at least thirty minutes. Sit down comfortably and relax. Breath deeply and slowly and as you exhale, imagine that all your worries, frustrations and problems are being expelled.*

*Now close your eyes and put your attention where your daydreams occur. This is the place between the eyes in the center of your forehead. It has many names, including the third eye. It actually forms a spiritual doorway to the heart of Soul. And the key to opening this door is unconditional love.*

*Imagine that way above you is a divine light. Open your heart with love to this light. It is the pure love of the divine source flowing down to you as a column of white light. It passes right through you and into the floor or ground. Continue to imagine this with as much clarity as possible. Can you also hear this light, maybe as the sound of rushing wind, or waves on a seashore, or even a high pitched flute or other woodwind instrument?*

*After several minutes begin to see your being become transparent. Imagine that this light from the divine source is purifying your being. And all obstacles to the flow of this light are being dissolved to the point that you become absolutely clear, as clear as crystal clear water. Hold this picture in your imagination for another few minutes and then, when you are ready, slowly return to this physical world. I specifically use these words "return to this physical world" as you have been on a short spiritual journey to a dimension higher than this Physical Plane.*

This exercise will greatly assist the flow of this beautiful divine love through your being. However, don't look for, or judge, your results. Just let it be and continue with your life. I suggest that you practice this exercise daily for between one and four weeks.

# Chapter 2.
# Overcoming Old Comfort Zones

## How to Gain Greater Freedom.

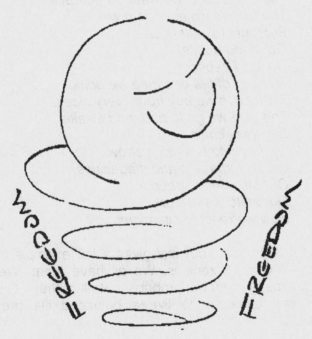

This is a very important topic, because we will never discover our mission in life, if our life is full of old comfort zones that restrict our freedom and talents. A comfort zone is something we do, or something we own, or a habit we have that allows us "to do it" or "to be it" without any effort or risk. We, as it were, do it blindfolded. Here are some typical comfort zones...

> *The house we live in.*
> *The job we do.*
> *The route we take to work.*
> *The clothes we wear.*
> *The time we eat.*
> *The food we eat.*
> *Our personality.*
> *The way we greet others.*
> *The expression we wear on our face.*
> *The friends we associate with.*
> *Personal relationships.*
> *Our good habits.*
> *Our bad habits.*
> *The cup of tea or coffee we drink.*
> *The shops we buy from every week.*
> *The time we go to bed, and awake.*
> *Our easy chair.*
> *Our favorite television show.*
> *Our newspapers and magazines.*
> *Our attitudes to people.*
> *Our attitudes to work.*
> *How we react to situations.*

The list is endless, but this gives a fair example of how simple a comfort zone is. We all have them. We may need some of them but probably not all of them. Only the ones that allow us to live a balanced life are truly necessary.

The problem with too many old comfort zones is that they can begin to place limitations on our abilities and freedom. Here is a short story to illustrate...

*There was a daughter at the bedside of her dying mother. Her mother was 89 years old and the daughter was 57. Every night in the week leading up to her mother's death, the daughter would visit and comfort her mother, and every night as the daughter left, the mother would whisper, "Be careful my love."*

*On the night before her mother's death she was walking from her mother's bedside, and she heard those immortal words "Be careful my love." Then the light shone into her life. She suddenly realized that for all of her life she had been careful. She had never taken any risks, she had never lived a little. She had never had any worthwhile experiences like her brothers, simply because she always tried to be careful. She realized that she was still single because she was being careful, that she was in the same old boring job since school because she was being careful, that she still lived with her mother because she was being careful, that her clothes were the same style as her mother's because she was being careful. The list was endless.*

*As this realization poured through her being she began to cry. However these were not the tears of sadness, but those of the sweet joy of Soul. She suddenly felt alive, filled with a new energy that she had never experienced since childhood. She turned to her mother and said, "No, mother I will not be careful. Tonight I feel like taking some risks in my life." Then as she descended the stairs she heard the immortal words again, "Be careful my love." However, it meant nothing to her this time, and with childlike curiosity, courage and adrenaline pumping, she went out into life, and took those risks.*

We need to ask ourselves some very direct questions and be honest with the answers. These questions go like this. When last did I take some risks in life? When last did I do something different? When last did I challenge my routine, or change my choice, or stand alone? Soul gets bored in the same old comfort zones day in, day out, year in, year out. If we stay in the same comfort zones for too long we are liable to experience massive change without warning. Soul must keep on moving, keep on experiencing.

Once we get stuck in a comfort zone, we, as it were, shut the door to Soul. But Soul gently pushes on the door to reconnect with its lower bodies. After all, Soul does own them. The more we resist change the more Soul pushes on the door. Suddenly this inner door will open, and the quantity of light that floods in will initiate a massive change in our life. We might not like the change; and that is why it is wise to keep on evaluating comfort zones to ensure we don't become stuck.

## Comfort Zones Are Our Teachers

Each comfort zone teaches us something about ourselves. It reflects an aspect of us. If this comfort zone keeps on reminding us of yesterday then we need to ask, "What is it teaching me about myself today?" Ask yourself what you are learning from each of these comfort zones. If the answer is nothing, then ask yourself if you still need this comfort zone in your life. Does it serve you or restrict you? Does it make you more than you were yesterday, or does it make you feel less than you were yesterday? Does it allow you to see the greatness in others, or does it show you their negative side?

As human beings we need a balance of new and old comfort zones to exist in. They enable us to live a reasonably balanced life. If we have no comfort zones then our life becomes like white water rafting, day and night. We soon cease to exist through stress. Life basically becomes too physical.

We need a balance between new comfort zones and old ones. A new comfort zone is one that we have newly acquired. By this I mean we have in some way done something different, stretched ourselves, challenged our abilities with a new situation, or taken some risks.

It is much like the mountain climbers who stretch their ability and challenge themselves beyond the normal level of challenge so that they can reach a higher peak on the mountain. When they reach the peak, and set down their tools, they then have reached a new comfort zone. They can relax, knowing that it has been a hard fight, but they have won. They have earned the comfort zone of rest, refreshment and reflection.

As Soul we need to truly strreeeetch our comfort zones from here to the far reaches of infinity, to the beautiful shores of the worlds of Soul. That is to say that no matter where we are in life we will feel comfortable from the vast inner heavens to anywhere on this physical planet. Old comfort zones lead to fear and worry when faced with new situations. New comfort zones fill us with excitement, anticipation and love when faced with something new and challenging.

Whenever we do something new in life all of the senses become enlivened and tuned in. As we become accustomed to this new situation, the senses go back to sleep until there is no perception of anything new. Our five senses are essentially the windows to Soul in this physical world. If what we see and do is the same every day then Soul gets bored as there is nothing new to experience.

## Becoming a Risk Taker

I believe that it is essential to take risks in life. Choosing to follow your mission in life is taking a big risk. It is risking being different than the masses of people. It is risking going against the expectation of others. It is taking the risk to stand up for individuality, to stand up for yourself. I believe that it is important to take at least one new risk a day. That is to say, do something new everyday. Break out of the set patterns that restrict, and make us less than we truly are. Here are some simple suggestions to overcome old comfort zones:

1. *Walk a different route than the usual one, and observe the detail in the scenery about you.*

2. *Try asking your physical body what it wants to eat.*

3. *Watch a different television program.*

4. *Talk with someone new today.*

5. *Tell someone about a good quality they have.*

6. *Drive a different way to work.*

7. *Observe a flower or a plant.*

8. *Look at the texture of the trees.*

9. *Take time to walk in nature.*

10. *Go to bed at a different time.*

11. *Write down some dreams you want to have occur.*

12. *Are your clothes boring? - Then buy some different ones.*

13. *Read a new style of book.*

14. *Buy a magazine you have never bought before.*

15. *Ask a neighbor if they need help in the garden.*

16. *Volunteer to wash a neighbor's car when you wash yours.*

17. *Offer someone fruit from your lunch box.*

18. *Give someone the benefit of the doubt for a change.*

19. *Buy someone a present when they least deserve it.*

20. *Look for the good in others.*

21. *Turn the bed to face a different direction.*

22. *Move the furniture around in the house.*

23. *Buy a different kind of music, and actually listen to it.*

24. *Make new friends this week.*

25. *Go on a holiday adventure.*

Some of these are easy to do and some are hard. This is just a short list. You can make a much better list for yourself. The important point to remember is that the little voice inside you which says, "Oh no, I can't do that." is the voice of the old comfort zones. It merges so totally and completely with ourselves that it is indistinguishable except for this little voice. Freeing ourselves of yesterday's restrictions also requires that we follow the golden key as mentioned in Chapter One: **"Look for love in every activity. Enter the activity with love and leave the activity glowing with love when we leave."**

I started by doing some small things first, like walking a different way to work, and as I did this I opened my eyes to take note of everything I saw and heard. I noticed the impressions I received and how alive I began to feel. Nothing in life is the same from moment to moment. Seeing these changes allows us to stay awake to life.

## Is the Comfort Zone Teaching You Something?

Another way to overcome old comfort zones is to determine if they are teaching us something useful. In the following chart I would invite you to write down your own list of comfort zones that cover your entire life. I have included a sample to help you on your way (on the next page). Use your Mission Journal for this exercise.

| Description of comfort zone | What am I learning from it? Is it useful? Do I want to change it? |
|---|---|
| *The job you do for a living* | Nothing. It is dead boring. I need to change it. |
| *The route you take to work* | Nothing. Just traffic jams, or maybe how not to get angry with other drivers. |
| *The clothes you wear* | They brighten my life, and other people's lives. I don't want to change these. |
| *The time you eat your food* | Nothing. Maybe I need to buy better food, which will give me more energy. Maybe I need to change my diet. |
| *The way you greet others* | The way I feel inside changes how I greet others, which affects the response I get from others. I need to start each day more positively. |
| *The expression you wear on your face* | I need to change it. It is too sad, but I need a reason to change |
| *The friends you associate with* | I learn nothing from them, except gossip. I need new friends!!!! |
| *The time you go to bed, and awake in the morning* | I need to get up earlier. I tried this before, and I was more alive, but I am lazy so I need a change here. |
| *Your easy chair* | I like my easy chair. It is my nest where I feel at ease with myself and the world. |
| *The newspapers, and magazines you read* | I need to change these to ones that more closely reflect where I want to go in life. |

## Two Spiritual Exercises

Now that we have completed our list of comfort zones I would like to invite you to do a short spiritual exercise. However, try and do this exercise at the time of day when you feel most relaxed as you indicated in the preparation section at the front of this book. The exercise goes as follows:

1. *Take one of the comfort zones from your list that you want to change. Maybe it is the job you feel you cannot leave, or the so called friends that just gossip and run you down all the time.*

2. *Sit yourself down comfortably, and take five deep breaths. Invite your body to become totally relaxed and at ease with itself.*

3. *Now imagine your comfort zone in the place where your daydreams occur, the place between your eyebrows at the center of your forehead. See the comfort zone in all its clarity, and recognize the reason why change is required.*

4. *Imagine a brilliant white light, similar to a powerful spotlight, clear away this image from your mind. This light comes from you as Soul. Use your imagination to see the white light clear away the image. If the image comes back, shine the light of Soul on it again to clear it away.*

5. *Imagine now that you have no limitations. Imagine what it must be like to be as free as an eagle soaring through the deep blue skies. See the freedom, then become this freedom. Keep this feeling of freedom in your imagination for at least five to ten minutes. Keep*

*on reinforcing it with the image of the eagle or something similar that represents freedom to you.*

6. *Hold this sense of freedom, and gradually return to the physical world.*

This exercise may need to be practiced everyday for about four weeks before the changes really begin to happen, but we are all individuals, and it will be different for each one of us.

Everything starts in the imagination and it will ultimately return there. No building, family, road, or event was ever brought forth except through the imagination. It is the imagination and our expectation that locks in or frees us from old comfort zones.

Here is another way to remove old comfort zones. It is another spiritual exercise for you to try. First of all pick three qualities of Soul which inspire you, that you feel will help you go beyond the restrictions of old comfort zones. Here is a list of some possibilities:

| | | |
|---|---|---|
| Divine Love | Compassion | Filled with Light |
| Wisdom | Understanding | Effort |
| Power | Infinite Viewpoint | Serene |
| Courage | Infinite Perception | Majestic |
| Knowledge | Harmony | Resourceful |
| Joy | Serving Life | Perceptiveness |
| Adventuresome | Abundance | Vitality |
| Strength | Masterful | Creative |
| Bold | Humility | Musical |
| Boundless | Timelessness | Knowing |
| Skillful | Laughter | Balance |
| Freedom | Beauty | Curiosity |
| Resilience | Clarity | Visionary |

*Now I invite you to prepare for contemplation by taking five deep breaths, making a request to your entire being to become relaxed. When you reach that state, close your eyes and imagine yourself being infused with light that comes from Soul. As this light shines through your being, picture yourself expressing that quality of Soul. So if you chose the quality of courage, picture yourself doing something courageous in life within a current comfort zone. You may imagine yourself having the courage to turn your back on friends who restrict your freedom, or the courage to resign from a miserable job. Continue with this in your imagination for about ten minutes. Then take five deep breaths and imagine that each breath infuses you with more of this quality.*

*As you open your eyes feel that you have become the expression of this quality. What you are doing, is pulling your inner being as Soul into your outer expression as self. The mind stretches to encompass this quality of Soul.*

## Taking Responsibility

There are many comfort zones that are cultural. We currently live in a world where it is fashionable to blame someone else for our misfortune, or blame the government for not doing something about the circumstances we find ourselves in. Basically laying the blame anywhere but at our own doorstep. It is comfortable to blame others, knowing that we don't have to do anything about our own situation. Thus we become lazy and bitter. Overcoming old stuck situations, no matter who caused them, begins by lovingly accepting that we allowed it to happen to ourselves. This may be difficult to accept for many. However, the truth is nothing can come to us unless we allow it through our own state of consciousness. If we allow our consciousness to soar into the high states of Soul, then many more beautiful and positive life-enforcing situations will flow our way. Hold our consciousness in the gutter of life where blame, hate, anger, vanity and attachment reside, and our low state of consciousness will embrace the situations that tend to mess up and threaten our life.

One of the best ways I know to get out of this blame culture is as follows:

1. First, acknowledge that there is an aspect of your life where you hold someone else responsible for messing it up. It does not matter how small. The idea is to free yourself completely from these false anchors that drag you down knowingly or not.

2. Then write down each situation that you find.

3. Finally find a good positive reason to forgive this person, and write down a short note of forgiveness in your Mission Journal. There are many good reasons for forgiveness, including...

> *I need my freedom back.*

> *I take back full responsibility for my life, therefore I control my destiny.*

> *I have gone beyond the energy that created this mess in the first place.*

> *I am greater than the problem, and in my greatness I set myself free of it.*

Some people even put the forgiveness message on a paper boat, and float it down the river at dawn. I am not suggesting you do this as it creates litter, but it is an example of the lengths some people need to go to when forgiving someone else for their misfortune. Even going up to the person in question, and apologizing to them for harboring these thoughts for so long is okay.

We need to make a statement that we accept full and total responsibility for our life. This is where we draw the line in the sand. This was very hard for me at first all those years ago as I was so accustomed to the church looking after me. They said they cared for me, and that Jesus was now responsible for the sins of my past, and that he had washed them all away. Having this drummed into the consciousness from an early age, it is hard to walk away from. Indeed I suffered a terrible fear complex after taking full responsibility for my life.

It was only by asserting that by being in control could I control my destiny. Then love and inspiration poured into my life. This responsibility was like being at the wheel of a car for the first time. I could go anywhere at anytime. Responsibility plus forgiveness equals freedom from the past, freedom to live in the now, and freedom to BE anything in the future. This freedom is yours by divine right. Don't let others steal it from you.

In closing I would like to touch on fear. It is something created by the mind in ignorance, and can lock us into uneasy comfort zones. Taken to extremes the mind will try to control and ultimately destroy that which it fears. For instance look at spiders. Harmless creatures, yet they die in the millions around the world everyday through fear. Unfortunately some people harbor this same fear of each other.

To me fear stands for **F**alse **E**vidence **A**ppearing **R**eal.

Love is the only thing that can melt away the fear that grips so many people's lives, and holds them in restriction. Ironically, fears usually come true. Dwell on the fear long enough, and it will simply happen in the same way a positive thing can happen. The divine essence of life will manifest whatever we strongly imagine. It does not question what we do, which is why we need to hold **one hundred percent** responsibility of our life, our thoughts, our feelings and our dreams.

# Chapter 3.
# Unfolding Your True Greatness

## How to Discover the True Greatness Within, and Flow It Into Your Life.

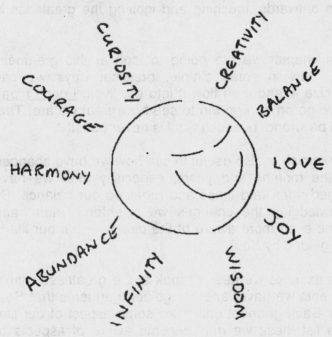

In finding our mission in life we are going to discover the true greatness that is within. Our mission is something that we have been preparing for since our first experiences in life. Every situation and event in our life up to now has served to help us reach this point in time.

Too often we take for granted the qualities and greatness that are within us. As we go through each experience in life we come out of it greater than before. This may not necessarily mean that we become wealthier, but rather that we have unwrapped more of Soul's qualities to bring us through the experience.

People and governments are always talking about making their country great, but too often they forget that it is people in themselves that become great. When the individual begins to express this greatness within, it then ripples outwards, touching and igniting the greatness in others.

In this chapter we are going to look at this greatness within, how in some simple, practical ways we can recognize it, and then flow it into our lives. I don't mean that we go on an ego trip to see how great we are. That would be wrong, because Soul is never boastful.

This exercise is also useful to see how we have changed over the months and years, especially after we have emerged from hard times and regained our balance. By acknowledging the changes we re-enforce them, and become even more aware of the direction that our life is being guided by Soul.

In this exercise we need to look at the greatness within, the talents we have, and the golden garments that Soul wears. Each garment enhances some aspect of our life. As we list these we may become aware of aspects of ourselves that we never knew we possessed. This is because **Soul is gently preparing the way ahead so that when we come to fly we already have the wings.**

## The Golden Garments of Soul

In your Mission Journal, create a list of your strengths and talents, like the list below.

| |
|---|
| I am a good listener. |
| I put others at ease very quickly. |
| I have a strong determination. |
| I am in good health. |
| I am perceptive. |
| I care about other people. |
| I am persistent and don't give up easily. |
| I can see the answers to problems easily. |
| I always see the best in others. |
| I am very loving. |
| and so on.................. |

Many people find it a good idea to add to this list every month. The list will usually dramatically expand once you begin to discover your mission in life.

In the next exercise I invite you to write down the points that others seem to like about you. This is more of an outside view looking in. An example is below...

| |
|---|
| My courage. |
| My ability to follow through on things I say I will do. |
| My directness. |
| My humor and jokes. |
| The fact that I never gossip. |
| The newspaper articles I write. |
| The team chats I give before the bowling matches. |
| How I make the bowling team feel better when we lose. |
| and so on.................. |

This next exercise goes back to the infinite qualities of Soul. If you were given a choice as to which of these qualities you would most like to express in your life, which five would you choose? Refer to the list on **page fifty three** of this book and feel free to to add to this list as it is personal and endless.

Now pick five qualities of Soul that you most want to express in your life. Write these down on a list and place it somewhere prominent like in your car, over the mirror at home, or even somewhere private at work.

---

The five qualities I most want to express in my life are...

1...                    3...

2...                    4...

5...

---

This is a very simple and effective exercise as it does not require a lot of effort, just conscious recognition when you see or pass the list during the day. However with time, you will begin to see opportunities to express these qualities and also notice these qualities emerging in you through your thoughts and actions.

## Where Is Your Point of Learning?

One of the greatest talents of Soul is the ability to learn. As we learn, we unfold more of the greatness within Soul and the more we unfold this greatness, the deeper our understanding of life becomes.

We are always responsible for every action we make, and we can see this from those aound us who are here to learn the lessons of life the hard way because they simply don't get it. However, it is not for anyone to judge another for all actions are relative to each other. It is not Soul that commits the acts of violence and atrocities in this world. It is the lower self. When people commit these acts they have cut themselves off from the Soul state, but what they do to others will come back to them. This is what the ancients called karma, the law of cause and effect.

We are here in this life to learn how to be the very best we can be. Learning to unfold this greatness is actually much more than understanding a new skill or language. The real learning comes when we align ourselves to Soul. This allows us to tap into more of the universal breath of God, or what we call divine love. The four ways that this learning occurs are through observation, adversity, good times and the adventures of Soul. As we are all individuals we learn in one or more of these ways. And we tend to cycle through these ways of learning as time goes by.

## Learning Through Observation

This is a smart, natural and simple way of learning. Simply put, it means seeing how it worked for someone else and repeating it. However, if taken too far, we fail to get the direct experience of a challenge.

## Learning Through Adversity

It is when things in life become difficult, when we have exhausted the common knowledge we have, that we begin to open up to the possibility of a force much greater then our physical, emotional or mental talents. Once we become aware of this we can use it to empower our life and move out of the difficult situation. It is in these times of great adversity that the majority of people grow the most spiritually. So often, after a time of adversity it is difficult to return to the old ways, the old routine, because we have outgrown the patterns of yesterday.

Imagine you are a farmer with a river running through your land. Adversity is within a situation where there has been no rain for months and the crops are dying. In desperation you remember that there are sleuth gates (water gates) from the river onto the land. You climb through the bushes, rocks and tangled fencing, and find a sleuth gate. With some effort it opens and water pours from the river onto the farm land and the drought disaster is over. For the future you decide to keep the sleuth gate ajar so that a little amount of the water trickles onto the land continually. This is how it is spiritually. The adversity creates the lack of rain. You have no solutions that readily work, so you try the sleuth gate, which is to tap into your true self, Soul. From Soul flows the solution. For the future, you keep this channel open so a little more of Soul is present in your daily life to a greater degree than before. The flow from Soul was always there. It was just that the pathway had become blocked by debris. This relates to us blocking the flow with an over inflated ego, unbalanced emotions, or a multitude of other attitudes.

## Learning Through the Good Times

This is probably the hardest way to learn, although it can be for most people a desirable state to be in. Basically, you have to find out what life is trying to teach you when the times are good and easy. Let us use the example of the farmer again. The rain is pouring down. The crops are watered. The sun also shines in the summer to ripen the fruits and vegatables. The frosts and snow occur in the winter to kill off the bugs, pests and germs. Everything is in balance. It is very hard for the farmer to spot the weakness in anything.

Relating this to your life, you would have to say to yourself, "What areas of my life am I weak in? What things can I do better? What was my last weak spot? Have I strengthened it or have I just moved on?"

## Learning Through the Adventures of Soul

This is the best way to learn, as it is essentially a kind of combination of the other three ways. The best way to sum up this way is by example. Image this. A friend of mine is a mountain climber. His goal is to reach the summit of the various mountains and rocks he climbs. While climbing on one rock he slipped and cut his arm badly, but his desire to reach the top was so strong that he had little time for the cut. He quickly cleaned the wound, tied a bandage around it and continued to climb the rock face. When he reached the top of the rock he relaxed and became inspired by another rock he saw from this great height. He descended from the summit to plan his next rock climb. When he reached the ground, he felt a sharp pain in his arm and remembered the bandaged wound. His wife inspected the wound and realized that one of the bones was broken.

Lets look at this. What my friend is doing is setting goals and challenges which are risky. He is taking a risk to step outside the comfort zone of common experience, and enter the world of inspiration and wisdom. He needs this wisdom to climb the rock face. Each rock he climbs is harder than the previous. In doing so he is overcoming fears, old limitations and embracing difficulties. He has little time for the bumps and bruises he collects along the way. Even broken arms must take a back seat to the goal. For he has chosen where his learning is going to come from and what he needs to learn in life to be the best that he can be.

With our mission in life we are choosing how and what lessons we will learn in life, so when the bumps and knocks come along they will be but a minor nuisance on our journey. How many times have we been so busy doing something, maybe cooking, working in the garden or working on the car? Then several hours later when we are relaxed we discover that we had earlier cut a finger or something similar, but we did not notice it at the time. So we must focus on the mission, and we will always be learning and expanding our consciousness in the direction that we are moving.

Contrast these examples to the type of person who sees no learning in life whatsoever. To this person life is here for the taking, to get what they can. They want to take life easy, letting others carry their burdens. Then the moment life takes a twist or turn, they are shaken to the core. They have become so uninvolved in life that they get whipped by life's tail. It causes drama and constant stress in their life because they have refused to learn. They have still to learn that life begins and flows from the loving Soul centered state.

## Mastering Life

There are three stages to mastering life and moving into this Soul centered state of greatness. It would be useful to check with yourself what stage you dwell in most. The most common stage is the "subjective experiencer". This is the person who is always the effect of situations, is always reacting to life. As we evolve we become the "observer" of these experiences. That is to say we have realized that we are not our emotional reactions. Neither are we the situations, or our intellect. We are an individual consciousness, so we now both experience and observe situations.

The final stage is when we become the "Soul centered being", that is to say we experience life with a Physical body that is at ease with itself, no matter what shape or size it may be. We experience higher emotions. This means our emotional state flows with more love and beauty rather than anger and lust or frustration. We are also centered in the here and now. We experience our highest mental faculty and we are aware of ourselves as Soul. From Soul's viewpoint, all of our lower bodies are dutiful happy servants.

The mind once again can be at ease with itself. No longer carrying the weight and responsibility of life on its shoulders, but instead being an equal co-worker and co-sharer with our entire being. This allows the greatness of Soul to soak into our entire being.

# Chapter 4.
# Catch the Vision
## How to Catch
## the Most Compelling Vision Within the
## Golden Heart of Soul

In the heart of Soul is the divine spark. This is the true origin of the life force within each individual. It is infused by the breath of the divine source. This is the source of our true greatness, and where the treasures of Soul are stored. It is in the heart of Soul that we find the compelling visions of our mission or missions in life.

At the start of this book there was a small dedication that I invited you to do if you were serious about finding your mission. The reason for this dedication was to mark a key turning point in your life. The moment you decide to find your mission, you will find that the entire universe begins to align itself with you. By this I mean that life begins to be charmed with incredible scenarios simply unfolding before your eyes. Whole series' of seemingly complex events seem to simply tumble into the correct formation for your benefit. Seemingly impossible situations work out for the best, and your immediate problems may begin to change for the better.

What is occurring spiritually, is that Soul is slowly taking charge of your life, and Soul works one hundred percent with Divine Spirit. This Divine Spirit is in everything, sustains everything, and is super intelligent. It of itself aligns with you to sustain and nourish your every effort to find your mission in life. It is likely that you will begin to experience a quickening in your life as if your own evolution is speeding up.

The moment we begin to understand our mission, a sense of elation and purpose will begin to well up within, and sweep through our life. The source of this elation and joy is in the heart of Soul. It is also true that you will begin to recognize how Spirit works, how it guides and helps you in every situation.

So to recap; Soul has a vision of your mission in life. Once you decide to find the mission, Soul works directly with Divine Spirit to orchestrate events and situations for your own highest good. If you do nothing in life, if you live within old comfort zones and take no risks to become great, then there can only be a limited number of Soul's qualities flowing in your life. However, your mission will immediately activate many qualities of Soul, and you will discover attributes and talents that will astonish and uplift you as you face the challenges ahead.

## Life Is a Perfect Mirror

Where you put your attention and attitude ultimately makes the difference between success and failure. If you are a thief, all you will see around you are things to be stolen. If you are a learner all you will see around you are things to learn. If you love the latest gossip you will always see people to gossip about. On the other hand if you are filled with love you will see people to be loved. If you are filled with wisdom you will see those who are in need of guidance, and if you are a success you will see opportunities to succeed. **Life unconditionally reflects what you are, and what you are is what you tend to see around you**.

I was in a discussion with a lady from Europe. We were talking about wealth. During the conversation she said that in her country what sickened her most was that ninety percent of the country's wealth was owned by just five percent of the population. As the conversation progressed, I suggested that wealth or success was not finite and limited to a chosen few. That anyone, if they chose to, could earn more, be more successful, and find new opportunities in life. That those five percent of the population were by and large people who had realized this fact. It was not an exclusive club, but open to all who wished to join.

The point I am trying to make is that attitude and attention can work for you or against you. This person had lived in poverty for most of her life because she believed that she was excluded from the five percent who owned ninetyfive percent. So it is important to realize that your personal circumstance does not restrict you from achieving your mission in life.

Your circumstances are perfect for you to discover your mission in life, and have never been better. Your mission in life is your greatest destiny, and you will find it as soon as you <u>are ready to accept it</u>. It may come all at once or in sections over a few days, months or even years. The vision comes to your realization in the degree to which you can accept, and work with it.

Imagine Soul. It is vast, deep, infinite, abundant, and wise beyond measure, but it now owns these five coarse vessels through which it experiences life in the lower worlds. In your heart you have a fabulous mission to embark upon, but your lower bodies are still struggling with one problem or another, and are not looking towards the heart of Soul. To impart to them this vision would scare the lower self, or it would be so much at variance with what is normal in life, that it would not be recognized. It would not adhere in the mind. However, the spiritual exercises that follow help to expand your awareness. Slowly, but surely, your consciousness becomes more Soul-like. From this expanded viewpoint you are able to see and work with Soul's vision.

## Your Mission Has No Boundaries

**A mission in life can be in any area of life such as family, personal, financial, business and leisure.** Soul's vision can also come to you in a number of ways. It does not have to be a bolt of light in the middle of the night, or a sudden realization while in the bathroom. It can be a most graceful realization, much like wandering along the beach on a summer's day, moving ever closer to the sparkling water's edge. Some people have received Soul's vision while driving their car to the point that the love flowing from Soul into their consciousness was so beautiful, so unconditional that they had to pull over, and stop the car.

Soul's vision of your mission in life is centered around three spiritual virtues of Soul. These are, the qualities of Soul, the areas of service, and the goal of the mission.

In practical terms it means the following:

## The Qualities of Soul

Soul's vision is vibrant because it is filled with divine love, and a number of other qualities of Soul, unique to each mission. So it is true to say that one way to discover your mission in life is to discover which qualities of Soul truly inspire you most. It is sometimes difficult to quantify the qualities of Soul until we have had some experience in life, usually adverse. It is under these conditions that true talents and true qualities emerge. As you begin to unfold the vision into your life all of the divine energy from the heart of Soul pours into these lower worlds. You will begin to find your life divinely blessed. Each quality of Soul greatly enhances your life as you steer in the direction of your mission.

## The Areas of Service

The next spiritual virtue of a mission is service. By this I mean giving to life without looking for something in return. Only Soul can truly give, and keep on giving, for it comes from the region of the infinite. If we look to life and expect that things ought to be there for us, or if we want endless welfare benefits, or expect others to do things for us all the time then we have sadly lost the plot. We are here in life out of our choice to give to life. This is why discovering Soul's vision is so important as it will lift us into the flow of life.

**The more we give to life the more we have to give**. This is a solid spiritual principle. The more we live in Soul's vision, the more life will serve us. We have to give, and give first to be able to receive. Take for example where I grew up in England. I would often observe two people selling flowers on a street corner. One is just selling flowers, he does okay and makes a living. The other person sells flowers, but he is living in Soul's vision. He is so vibrant in doing a part of his mission that more people want to buy flowers from him than from the other guy. As he sells each flower the love that flows from each sale blesses each buyer, so they come back all the more. This is why his business literally blossoms.

## The Goal of the Mission

There can be one or many goals in a mission. This is the physical event that best expresses the vision. We can change the goal at any time to suit our better understanding of the vision.

Usually, I find that the more we live in the vision the better we know and understand it, and the goals tend to clarify as we progress through life. It is a good idea to make short, medium and long term goals to represent the vision. Soul crafts the vision out of everyday stuff like problems, relationships, anxieties, failures, opportunities and successes. Everything is available to Soul as the master crafter.

Soul can illuminate a vision in the imagination in an instant to match a changed circumstance. So whether you are involved in a minor car accident, a dispute at work or you win some money at a casino, nothing goes unnoticed by Soul. In fact Soul usually orchestrates the changes in your life. This particularly occurs with a greater frequency when you are seeking Soul's vision or actually performing your mission in life.

As mentioned before, there are many ways in which we can catch the vision. The process starts with Soul infusing the spark of God into a vision. This vision or picture is held in the heart of Soul. However, the lower consciousness, the mind and below has to accept that it has a destiny in life, that it has something to give back to life. Once this acceptance has occurred, Soul will work with Divine Spirit, the raw materials in your life, and with your night time dreams. Basically every aspect of your being and life is used by Soul. It looks for the best way to lovingly share this vision.

Soul knows that the mind cannot always accept the beauty, wonder and splendor of the vision, so Soul often works in the dream state to gently implant dreams that begin to turn your life around to point you in the direction of your mission. This turning around process may be necessary if your current direction in life is opposite to the direction of your mission. This was certainly true in my situation. Many people experience this as a turning point or crossroads in life.

Once we are facing in a direction relatively close to that of our mission, Soul will begin to accelerate the recognition process in the mind. What occurs here is that Soul works with Divine Spirit to orchestrate and unfold millions of beautiful golden steps. Each step draws us a little closer to the heart of Soul. We effectively begin to merge more and more with Soul, and thus become more

Soul-like. It is during this state that we begin to feel and notice **golden moments**. Simply put, this is when Soul selects an outer picture in our life and illuminates it above all else. This could be in a conversation we overhear as background noise, when all of a sudden a word or phrase stands out over everything else, or we see a picture and feel strangely attracted to it, or smell an odor that reminds us of something we cannot put our finger on. We may find ourselves thinking something, then someone on the radio mentions that very thing or something similar. These are all golden moments. We need to write each one down and also write down what we were thinking or doing at that time.

Each golden moment represents a moment when a related picture or the actual vision in the heart of Soul resonates with an incident in our daily life. It is like an opera singer who can shatter a glass with her voice. It only shatters at a particular pitch, but we never know what that pitch is until we put the glass in front of the radio and listen to the opera, and then we'll know at what point the glass shatters.

This is like life. The more we get involved in it the more we have opportunities for Soul to match its vision with an outer situation. It is common to experience an upliftment in life during one of these moments. Our heart usually opens and divine love seems to pour into our life from Soul. For that brief moment we experience greater degrees of Soul Realization.

## Introducing the HU

I would now like to explain about some of the spiritual exercises to follow.

- 76 -

Divine love, this sweet essence of life, pours through our being at all times. It comes from the heart of the divine source, right into the heart of Soul, and then into our lower bodies. This divine love can be seen as light and heard as sound. The more divine love flowing through our life, the more effective we become in life. Divine love is the loving life force that sustains all of life. Our pure essence, Soul, is constantly bathed in this divine love. So life is about becoming more of our divine self, which is divine love. The more we become like Soul, the more effective our life becomes. The more effective we are in life, the more effective we become in our mission in life. Simply put, the greater the divine love in our heart, the brighter, more joyful and more adventurous our mission in life becomes.

The question is, how do we go about bringing more divine love into our life? How do we become more Soul-like? Well, there are many ways; however, the common theme is always about selfless giving. Here are a few examples.

*Doing a kind deed for someone.*
*Acting in an unselfish way.*
*Doing everything with love in your heart.*
*Looking for the best in everyone you meet.*
*Seeing the divine purpose in all life.*
*Being grateful for all things in life.*
*Living with great expectation.*
*Looking for the blessings of life.*

Many Eastern teachings have taught the use of mantras to become more loving and Soul-like. The word AUM is a good example of one of these mantras. It can be chanted to raise the consciousness. Essentially, everything in life is crafted from the light and sound, the twin aspects of divine love. Every atom and molecule, the building blocks of physical matter, have a rate of vibration. The faster they vibrate the finer and more fluid they become. The slower they vibrate the more dense and solid they become. When people sing the word AUM it resonates within the Mental body and makes the connection via the chakra less dense. This in turn allows a more fluid flow of energy between the Mental body and the physical self. Over time more of the finer qualities of their mental self are expressed in their physical being. They can become more loving, more stable, etc.

There are a number of sounds that affect our inner self in many different ways. Some sounds can make us more docile, some can make us angry, some make us bold. A typical example of sounds that make people bold are the chants used by the Army. It strengthens emotions and focuses the mind on the job to be done.

There is a word, a sound that is above and also within all sounds. It is the sound of Soul, the sound of divine love. This sound is HU. This word is a very pure sound, and when you sing this word HU, it will fill you with divine love. It lifts the consciousness into the heart of Soul and then expands the heart of Soul into the divine source.

HU is pronounced as "hue" on a long outward breath gradually trailing off. Then you breath in, and sing HU again on a long outward breath. You will need to experiment with various tones until you find a tone that most suits you. When you sing HU, place your attention where your daydreams occur in your imagination. Then imagine that you are the radiant, loving heart of Soul. As you sing HU on the outward breath, imagine that the light within shines ever brighter, making you ever more radiant.

It is as if the sun comes from behind the clouds every time you sing the HU, and everything is brighter than before. There is a beauty in everything, and the beauty is a reflection of you. Imagine the light of Soul-like a billion suns, radiating unconditional love. As you continue to flow with your imagination, reflect on the greatness of Soul and wonder at the source of the light. Your true nature in all its beauty, wonder and love always shines brigher after each HU.

When you sing this word HU try to sing it with sweetness, beauty and love. A way to inspire this is by putting your attention on something you feel love for or find beautiful or sweet or something that just fills you with wonder. I like to put my attention on the heart of Soul or on the divine source as this just fills me with such gratitude for life. **Treat the HU as your sacred and personal love song from the heart of Soul to the divine source.**

The HU song can be done silently or out loud anywhere and anytime. After you have finished singing the HU don't mentalize or try to analyze the results. Singing the HU is all about becoming more Soul-like. If you are faced with a difficult problem, singing HU with love will allow you to see the situation with the eyes of Soul. This higher viewpoint will allow you to take better steps in the face of adversity. **The sound of the HU not only lifts your consciousness, but that of everything around you.** **The HU is really life transforming** **in every sense of the word.**

### Singing HU With a Partner

It is perfectly fine to sing the HU with your partner. However, your partner should be a willing participant and know exactly what the HU is all about. In this case, one person should start and the other can join in. Just let the HU song keep rolling. Also pay no mental attention to when the other person starts or stops each HU.

## The Length of the HU Song

The length of the HU song should not be more than twenty minutes. It is like pouring water into a cup. At some point the cup will overflow so it needs to be emptied. It is the same with spiritual exercises. Your being becomes filled with awesome light during the HU song. It then becomes necessary to allow this light, this divine love to flow out into life. As always it comes back to love. Doing something with love that serves life keeps the light flowing through your being. And it can be as simple as saying "Hello" or offering to help someone with their shopping or just going about your day gently shining the love in your heart to all.

## How to Conclude the HU Song

After finishing the HU song, allow several minutes to experience these higher states of Soul Realization. Allow the imagination to soar deeper into the light, towards beauty and love. Listen for the inner celestial sounds of divine love as mentioned earlier. See how these sounds unfold as you place Soul's attention upon them.

## The Sound and Light in the HU

Some people can sing the HU, and immediately see the light and hear the sound; the twin aspects of divine love. The sound is usually heard as flutes, woodwind instruments, winds, water, waves, high pitched sounds, humming and more. These are the sounds of divine love resonating on the various inner planes, bathing them and your inner being with love. With the sound comes the light, and it shines in many colors. The color and intensity of the light you see depends on your spiritual awareness. It can appear as a star, a point of light, bright flashes of light all around you, or even direct and constant perception of the light. The brightness of the light increases as you move on up through the lower worlds. Then, as you move into the higher worlds of Soul, the light takes on an incredible brilliance and vitality. Here, the colors tend to sparkle and shine with great intensity.

This HU sound is found in the high spiritual worlds above the Soul Plane. If it helps, imagine that singing HU works much like striking a tuning fork on a piano. Immediately, a particular piano note comes to life. Soul is like that piano note. So Singing HU is our outer tuning fork. Unlike the word AUM, the HU sound tunes all of our lower vessels into the splendor of Soul, and the divine source of all life. Each time we sing HU, Soul's outer garments; the Physical, Emotional, Mental and Etheric bodies, become infused with more divine light. It is a light beyond description, an illumination beyond comparison. Singing HU on a regular basis will mark the dawning of a brighter future for you.

## Spiritual Exercises to Catch Soul's Vision

The following exercises which use the HU allow you to directly perceive Soul's vision. This results in you having one or more of these spiritual experiences, depending on what you are spiritually tuned into. You might want to write this list out in your Mission Journal.

1. You see Soul's vision clearly.
2. You have a dream where you see Soul's vision.
3. You know what your next step in life is.
4. A gentle knowingness about the future enters your life.
5. A feeling of splendor enters your life.
6. You get dream guidance about your next step or mission.
7. You experience **golden moments** to illuminate the way.
8. You have a strong feeling about a new direction.
9. You overcome a difficult indecision and move forward.
10. You see changes needed in your lifestyle to progress.
11. You understand your purpose in this life.
12. Things begin to work out in your life.
13. An interesting challenge arrives in your life.

While I have listed here possible ways to catch Soul's vision, we can never limit or dictate to Divine Spirit how it will occur. It is Soul working with Spirit that decides, and what it decides will always be the very best and for our highest good. Guaranteed!

**READ THROUGH THE FOLLOWING TECHNIQUES, THEN PICK THE ONE THAT IS THE MOST INSPIRING.** Write the chosen exercise down in your Mission Journal. If you can, write it out three times to become familiar with it. Although some people get results almost immediately, a month is probably the minimum time required.

If after six months you have no results, take a break of several weeks or even months. Then go back to Chapter One, and follow through again to Chapter Four. However, pay more attention to Chapter Two on Comfort Zones, spending more time on the exercises. Remember a lack of perceived progress just means that **Soul is still working with your entire being, preparing it to receive the vision**. So don't look on it as a failure, but as extended preparation.

It is also a good idea to keep up with the HU song spiritual exercise. This will allow you to continue to unfold spiritually.

**Important note:**
As soon as you Catch the Vision with the chosen technique immediatly proceed to Chapter Five.

## How to Catch Soul's Vision
## Technique 1.

# The Puzzle Box

You will need a packet of thirty or so index or address cards for this technique, as mentioned at the beginning of this book.

Make a cardboard box with a slot in the top large enough to put one of these cards through. You need to be able to seal it up so that it won't open accidentally. I suggest that you cover this box in nice wrapping paper that is pleasing to the eyes, especially if the box has advertizing on it.

Irrespective of how intelligent you may be, the mind is a tiny vessel compared to Soul. If the mind were to experience the brilliance of Soul's light it would burn the mind to ashes. That is why there are inner planes or worlds to transform the light into a lower vibration for each of your bodies, including the Mental body. So here we have Soul. It is vast, unlimited, abundant, above time and space, filled with love, and tuned to the divine current of life. At lower vibrations we have our lower bodies each tiny in comparison to Soul.

How does Soul communicate to its lower self in a clear, and concise way that does not get garbled as in some dreams? Well, one way is to collect all the little bits of guidance that comes from Soul and reassemble them into the big picture; the vision in the heart of Soul. This Puzzle Box Technique does just that, and it works like this:

Look at your calendar, and ask yourself how long it will take to discover Soul's vision of the mission. Then look at each month onward from today, and go with whatever month feels best. It may be one month or six; twelve months or longer. Then ask yourself, if this number of months came from your emotional self or from Soul? When it comes from Soul, there is a sense of illumination, a nice light feel to it.

Now you need to mark this date down in your Mission Journal, with words like, "I will know my mission in life by" *(followed by the date selected).* Then take one of the yellow cards and write on it in a bold marker in large letters "I will know Soul's vision by" *(followed by the date selected).* Place this card somewhere prominent where you will constantly see it, like by the telephone, or over the television or on the car dashboard. This is your declaration of intent. *(If it is difficult to put the yellow cards up because of discretion, place them in your Mission Journal. Then open it at least twice a day and read them.)*

Now take another of the yellow cards and write down on it in large letters "If I knew my mission in life, what would it be?" Place this yellow card in another prominent place in the house, or car, or at work.

## Then Each Morning

Go to the place where you do your contemplation.

Spend a few minutes relaxing, so that your body feels at ease with itself, then close your eyes. Now allow your imagination to wonder about your fabulous mission ahead, what it might be.

Imagine that feeling of expectation, what it feels like, and allow that warm feeling, like a midday sun, to flow into your heart. With this same feeling of loving expectation begin to sing HU for approximately ten minutes. Sing the HU as a love song from the golden heart of Soul to the divine source.

When you are ready, close the contemplation with a dedication, something like this: *"I am Soul therefore I am infinite, talented, creative and courageous. I sail towards my destiny in every moment of every day."* Then when you are ready, gently open your eyes to this physical world.

When you use a dedication it's important to try to truly feel the essence and loving power within it. It needs to mean something to you, else it becomes as empty words. Take time to sing the HU with love in your heart, remember there is no hurry.

### And at Midday

Do dedication that builds on the morning's dedication. It could go something like, *"I Am Soul therefore I am free and boundless. Everything in life lovingly guides me towards my mission."* As you say this allow your imagination to drift into the infinite, to see beauty and things that are boundless, like expressions of nature.

### Then at Night

Your dedication here could go something like, *"I am Soul therefore I am grateful for the guidance I receive, seen and unseen. May I continue to receive guidance as night falls. May the light within me guide and illuminate my mission in life, for I know that each step I take is a golden step towards a wonderful mission"*. As you go off to sleep hold an attitude of great expectation, much like a child on Christmas eve.

## And Each Day - Collect Golden Moments

You need to carry at all times at least twelve yellow cards, and when a golden moment occurs, write it down on a yellow card. Remember a golden moment is when Soul highlights something that stands out of the ordinary background to life. So this could be significant dreams, words on an advertizement, a newspaper title, a conversation you overhear when one or two words stand out, the writing on the side of a truck or van, a phrase or picture in a television advertizement.

Anything goes. Whatever stands out for you above the normal level of information hitting your consciousness. Write down all these golden moments, and what made them stand out. Try not to explain in too much detail where a short sentence or title will do. Here are some real life examples...

1.  *A sticker on a truck said Lake View Homes, and I had been thinking that morning about moving to a new house, and what place would be ideal.*

2.  *I had a dream that I was inventing something to help blind people see. It was a ball on the end of their white stick, and it meant that they could tell the sidewalk from the main road. It seemed so exciting, and helpful.*

3.  *As I walked in the forest, I looked up and saw a pine tree like a needle pointing towards the North Star. It was just a fabulous sight. I had seen a*

picture the day before about stars at night over a forest.

4.   When I went to pay for my food, I noticed that the checkout girl was wearing the same T-shirt as me with the logo "Save the Whale". I had completely forgotten about this logo, and suddenly it meant something to me. I remembered why I originally bought it, but I had lost enthusiasm over the years.

5.   I have seen a picture of a dolphin in my dreams twice in the last two nights. In each dream I seem to be feeding the dolphin with lettuce. What hits me is how happy the dolphin is after eating the lettuce.

6.   We were trying to find a house, and drove down a road for miles. At the end of the road there was a billboard poster with the sign, "Are you doing it backwards?" I did not see the rest of the poster, just those words stood out for me. I knew it was connected with the way I was driving my life.

7.   In the last week four people have written notes to me on purple paper at work. It would seem that by sheer divine coincidence, each note was connected with an event that needed to be organized.

8.   I was in the aircraft when they announced that food would be served in ten minutes. As I heard the announcement I looked out the window, and saw a giant sandwich. I looked again, and realized that it was just a big cloud. I had been thinking about expanding my sandwich food business into the next state.

9. *I had an amazing dream that the world had ended, but it was all okay as a new world was born. I then realized that this was me letting go of the world controlling me, and creating a new world that was me. The first thing I saw in the new world was a factory I owned producing something vital for this new world.*

10. *I keep hearing on the news the word "countryside". I don't know the connection, but I am writing it down.*

11. *My friends keep on telling me how good I am at listening to others, and making people feel good about themselves. Today was another example of this. I guess that I have not really paid much attention to this talent.*

12. *I have always been good with plants, and recently a friend asked me where I get my plants from. I told her that normally people give them to me, and ask if there is anything I can do for this plant. I usually have them thriving within a few weeks. I guess that it has just dawned on me how good I am with plants. I used to think that people simply did not care for them, but maybe there is more to this than meets the eye. Maybe I need to pay more attention to how I heal plants.*

So as you can see, it is quite simple to note down these golden moments onto the yellow cards, then place them into the box, and forget all about them.

## The Date to Discover Your Mission Arrives

You should by now have collected a large number of yellow cards. If there are only a few in the box, one of three things may have occurred...

(a)    You set the date to open the box too soon, so reset it to a future date, and continue collecting the cards.

(b)    You are missing golden moments. Maybe life is too complex, maybe you need to relax more. Look at possible reasons why you may not be seeing these moments, because they occur all the time. So you need to re-evaluate, then try again.

(c)    You only needed a few cards to catch the vision of Soul.

## Open the Box

Open the box, and empty these yellow cards onto a table. Remember each card is a part of the vision from Soul. What you have is a picture puzzle to be assembled.

Now read what is on each card, and group each card into related topics. Read the first card which (for example) is about ladders and put it down. Then read the next which is about food, so put that next to the ladders card. The next card you pick up may be about steps, so you could put it on top of the ladders card, as it connects. The next card is about feeding plants, so place that on top of the food card, and so on. Keep looking for golden threads running between the cards. It may not be obvious at first. You could eventually end up with twenty or more groups of cards or just two or three. It will be different for each person.

## Begin to See the Vision

Now separate the largest group of cards, and put the rest back into the box. This large group represents many small pictures of Soul's vision. Spread them out on the table in front of you, and write down in your Mission Journal what was the association title for this group of cards, for example "climbing ladders".

## We Then Ponder

Now take some time, and ponder on the picture these cards construct. Then like a master puzzle builder begin to sift through these cards looking for the connecting golden threads. By this I mean find out what connects them with you, and with your destiny. Ask yourself questions like; What illuminates this card or that card? What style of life do these cards inspire? What kind of feeling do you sense? What pictures do they carry? What changes do they signal? What freedom do they inspire? What qualities of Soul do they highlight?

How are they all linked together? The picture is all there so persevere, and you will catch the vision.

## And Finally

Write down in your Mission Journal in as much detail as possible what you have discovered, what you see the vision as. Remember, you do not need to in any way limit yourself to what has gone before. You were infinite before. You are infinite now, and you will continue to be infinite afterwards. You have no limitations. If you sweep roads now, and you have an impression that you will fly an aircraft, then you should never put it out of your imagination because it sounds too fanciful. You need to keep with it. Keep faith with Soul. **Do this, and you honor yourself.** Soul will, and does work with Divine Spirit to orchestrate events in life to bring you to the doorsteps of your mission, and it will do it via the best route, for your highest good, by whatever route that you happen to take.

If these cards do not make a picture immediately, try sleeping on it. This means giving the subconscious an instruction before we sleep to illuminate Soul's vision to us via these cards, and to give the answer by the morning. For example, *"I ask my subconscious to illuminate Soul's vision of my mission in life via these cards by the time I awake in the morning."* Then go to bed with great expectation.

In the morning have a quick browse over the cards, and write down in as much detail as you can the impressions you get from them. Remember, detail at this stage is very important, even if it is just an impression you need to write down what it may mean in as much detail as possible.

Step by step you will begin to witness Soul's vision being illustrated in front of your very eyes.

## How to Catch Soul's Vision
## Technique 2.

# The Puzzle Box of Wisdom

This technique is almost identical to the previous one, however there is an important difference. With this technique you are going to connect some common everyday wisdom to try and help guide your attention to the brightest possible vision. You will need for this, a good book of verse. This can be anything from the *Bible*, the *I Ching* or any book of inspired verse or poetry. The more uplifting the better. This is extremely important. Ideally, it should have short verses in it as you need to copy a few of these down. You still need the packet of index cards.

Now follow all the steps as described in the previous Puzzle Box Technique except for the following changes. Read the previous technique and add these paragraphs under the appropriate headings.

### And Each Day - Collect Golden Moments

Before you put the golden moments into your collection box, put a title on the top saying **"Golden Moment"** and date them. Then on the back put a title called **"Wisdom"** and open your chosen book of verse at random. Select a verse blindly with your finger, and write this on the back of the card under the heading, Wisdom. Remember to always imagine that as Soul, you select the page and verse, and never hesitate. Just do it as if you already know what verse to select. All you have to do now is place it into the box as before.

When the date arrives to discover the vision lay the cards out on the table as in the previous exercise.

## We Ponder

On the back of these cards is your very own wisdom verse. Use these to help focus and clarify the vision. Maybe you can turn all the cards over and see what the wisdom verses say, or flip over one or two wisdom verses to help focus the picture. Look at the date, maybe this is important too. You need to keep on writing down impressions you receive from Soul. Remember, you are always getting closer and clearer with every action you take. Soon the vision will emerge.

## And Finally

You can use your reservoir of wisdom notes to ponder upon before you sleep. Remember, as Soul you have chosen these as fragments of Soul's vision. Each wisdom verse or golden moment contains within it the seeds of your mission.

In the morning as you awake, gently go back to the moment before you became conscious in the physical world and ponder on the impressions you received. It could be through dreams or nudges or words. Write them down in as much detail as possible.

## How to Catch Soul's Vision
## Technique 3.

# Soul's Golden Door

Soul knows everything, and can be anything. In your heart is a beautiful divine vision beyond compare. Something that can illuminate your life so completely and totally. However, to tap into this you must be looking in the right direction, and you begin to turn yourself into the right direction by acceptance of this **greater destiny you have.** Then all you have to do is ask the right questions.

There are basically two types of questions; the type that complain, and the type that inquire. All questioning comes from the mind, not Soul. So let's look at these types of questions.

To complain in this context we could say something like:

> *Why can't I find a direction in life?*
> *Why aren't things working out?*
> *Why can't I master my destiny?*

The common thing in a complaint is the word "why". The energy for this word is usually negative, putting the blame elsewhere rather than taking responsibility.

The inquiring mind asks the question this way:

> *What is my next step in life?*
> *Is there something I am missing here?*
> *How can I master my destiny?*

Do you notice how the same questions have a much more bountiful energy about them while holding the reigns of responsibility? The point at where you focus your responsibility is the point at which you will find your next step. An inquiring mind works closely with the curiosity of Soul.

## The Morning Spiritual Exercise

*The Golden Door technique works with the inquiring mind and goes like this. In the morning, and as early as possible sit down in contemplation for just ten minutes. Take time to become completely relaxed and at ease with yourself. Next, close your eyes and lovingly put your attention at the place between your eyes where your daydreams occur. Now as a love song from the heart of Soul to the divine source, sing this beautiful word HU five times. As you sing HU on each outward breath, imagine the sound uplifting you, taking you to a higher level. And on the fifth HU you become the golden sparkling heart of Soul.*

Then repeat this declaration three times and lightly reflect on what your next step might be.

*"I am Soul, and as a divine spark of God I am ready to take my next step in life."*

Imagine a golden door between the mind and Soul. From the mind's viewpoint look down a short dark corridor towards this golden door. Where the door meets the ceiling, wall and floor you can see shafts of majestic white light reaching out towards you as you move towards the door.

Hold this image in your imagination for a minute or so with great expectation. Then see in your imagination this door bursting open and flooding your mind, your entire being, with the divine majestic light of Soul. Feel or see thousands of images flood into your mind and into your being, either as points of light, showers of sparkles, or a column of light.

Hold in your imagination this illuminated state for a few minutes. Then with gratitude in your heart, open your eyes, and continue your day.

**Then at Midday**

Remember to ask yourself the questions:

> *What is my mission in life?*
> *How can I take my next step?*

Find some time to ponder on this as you ask the questions. I like to walk by the rivers and lakes when asking these Soul searching questions. Anything that is natural is great as it reminds you of your true nature, which is infinite.

**And in the Evening**

In the evening before you go to bed I suggest an evening salutation as follows:

> *"I am Soul, a divine spark of God. May the majestic light of Soul pour through me and into my life. I ask to see, and be guided through my next step in life, so I may see my mission."*

## Then Every Night

Write a line in your journal with the date, and the question, "What is my mission?", and a new line with the question, "What is my next step?"

Now an important step is this. As you fall off to sleep ponder on what your mission in life is, "What is the destiny of my greatness? What is my mission in life?" Gently ponder on these questions, and hold a knowingness that you are moving ever closer to the answer. During the day write down moments in your life that are golden - out of the ordinary. Then at the end of each day browse through these moments, while pondering on the questions, "What is my next step? What is my mission?" Make sure you put any answers or impressions you receive in your Mission Journal.

Whether you see your next step or the entire mission will depend on your state of consciousness, but the idea is to be grateful for any change, for it will always be a change for the better.

Repetition is the key to success here. You may need to keep on working with this technique three times a day and everyday for a minimum of thirty days for any degree of success. **Every time you make the declaration or ask the question you are strengthening the link between Soul and your whole being.**

The weak link between Soul and the mind has been schooled into some people's mind through years of mis-information and illusion. It may take time to work, but it will work, and when it works you will be astounded by the simplicity of it all. You will be able to ask any question and get an immediate answer from your true self, Soul.

The more you begin to work in this Soul Realized state the more Soul-like you will become.

## And Finally

In your Mission Journal write down the answers you receive from Soul. It does not matter if it seems impossible, write it down. This will either be your next step in life or an accurate description of your mission in life.

How to Catch Soul's Vision

Technique 4.

# **Majestic Qualities of Soul**

The technique I would like to share with you here is simple, yet very powerful. Soul has an infinite number of qualities, and Soul's vision is infused with a number of these qualities. I would like you to refer to your list of Soul's qualities in your Mission Journal, or use the list on **page fifty three.** Look at this list and add any further qualities you may have discovered. Then in your Mission Journal write down the six qualities that truly inspire you. By this I mean they catch your attention in some positive way and seem exciting or fascinating. It is a sure bet that the qualities that light up for you are expressed in Soul's vision.

Now that you have selected six qualities that really light up for you write them down in your Mission Journal at the tips of a six pointed star as below:

- 100 -

These six qualities are the keys to Soul's vision. There is a short contemplation exercise that goes with this to unlock the actual picture in the heart of Soul.

In the morning or as early as possible try the following spiritual exercise.

## The Spiritual Exercise

*Sit down, close your eyes and take a few moments to invite your entire being to become relaxed and at ease with itself.*

*Then in your own time lovingly put your attention at the place between your eyes where your daydreams occur. Now as a love song from the heart of Soul to the divine source, sing this beautiful word HU five times. As you sing HU on each outward breath, imagine the sound uplifting you to a higher level. And on the fifth HU, imagine you become the golden sparkling heart of Soul.*

*Now ponder on each of the six qualities of Soul. What outer expression of yourself can you see that matches each or one of these qualities? Take your time as you roam and explore the fullness of each quality. Just let the imagination wander like on a beautiful carefree summer's day. Let your imagination explore and gently come to rest on any image that seems to reflect a quality of Soul you have chosen. Your imagination is occurring at a very high level of consciousness, above the mind, and therefore has no constraints. It is unlimited so don't restrict yourself.*

*As you find an image that lights up, note it down in your mind. Do this for about ten minutes. At the end of your contemplation come back easily and smoothly. Open your eyes, and describe in your Mission Journal as clearly as possible the images that were lighting up for you in your contemplation.*

*Allow your five senses to explore this quality as well so you can see how it affects them. If an image inspires you it almost certainly will ignite one or more of your senses.*

Do this exercise every day for thirty days, each time writing down in your Mission Journal a clear description of what your imagination inspired in you. It does not matter if your imagination keeps on bringing back the same imagery, just write it down.

After thirty days, pick the image that inspires you more than anything else and write down why you picked it. This image is Soul's vision, or your impression of it, or even your next step. It does not matter. You can always come back later for the next step or to clarify the vision.

## How to Catch Soul's Vision
## Technique 5.

# <u>A Stylish Story</u>

If you like stories, and you are a good observer of life and styles of life then this technique would work very well for you. It is based on the spiritual principle that everything in your life has been preparing you for your mission.

So what I am going to ask you to do is become the observer of your life, and go back to childhood in your imagination. Observe how life has changed since then.

As the observer I want you to write down your life story as a short series of stories. Each describing a stage and a style of your life. The first exercise is to highlight all the stages in your life where there has been a distinct style change. Then write about each of these stages of your life as short, but detailed stories.

The next part of this exercise is to read through each of the short stories from the past and note down what the event was that triggered the change in your lifestyle,

The last part is a spiritual exercise. Try doing this exercise when you are most inspired.

### <u>The Spiritual Exercise</u>

*In your own time lovingly put your attention at the place between your eyes where your daydreams occur. Now as a love song from the heart of Soul to the divine source, sing this beautiful word HU five times. As you sing HU on each outward breath, imagine the sound uplifting you, taking you to a higher level. And on the fifth HU, imagine you become the golden sparkling heart of Soul.*

*In this expanded state of consciousness, where you have no limits and no boundaries, imagine you have a golden pen, and you are going to continue to write the next short story about your life. As you begin to write, imagine your surroundings. Begin to change to reflect exactly what you write, so if the scenery does not seem right you know immediately, and can change it. Focus on the style of life that is important to you, the values and qualities you enjoy, and the things you can do that serve life and make a difference for the better.*

Do this exercise for up to thirty minutes in any one day, but do explore the next stage of your life fully. Finally, in your own time gently come back from these inner worlds, and open your eyes. After each contemplation period write down in your Mission Journal the story so far.

A key point here is this. As the story unfolds, ask yourself, "How am I serving life? How am I making a difference for the better?" If you cannot see this in the story then change it to include this. Finally, ask yourself, "What is it about this style of life depicted in the story that I like? What values have become more important and what qualities are illuminated in this story?" It is a very important detail so write it down.

It could be that every time you use this technique you bring back a beautiful story of a future stage of your life. Each story may be worthy of a hero, however after thirty days, pick one that really inspires more than the rest.

How to Catch Soul's Vision

Technique 6.

# **Steps of Gold**

This is a lovely technique which I have used many times. I would suggest that the best time to do this exercise is just before you go to sleep. This is very important to its success.

## The Spiritual Exercise

*Lay down on your bed, close your eyes and relax for a few minutes.*

*Then in your own time lovingly put your attention at the place between your eyes where your daydreams occur. Now as a love song from the heart of Soul to the divine source, sing this beautiful word HU five times. As you sing HU on each outward breath, imagine the sound uplifting you, taking you to a higher level. And on the fifth HU, imagine you become the golden sparkling heart of Soul, filled with majestic light.*

*Now let your imagination play and wander in this beautiful state of consciousness, and if necessary continue to sing the HU silently to yourself.*

*As you explore your consciousness and the imagery let it drift to a waterfall on the Soul Plane. A truly beautiful waterfall. The waters are falling from as high as the sky into a pool so deep and blue. As the water splashes into this pool, rainbows of light shower down upon you. Look for the beauty, and feel your heart open.*

*As it does, imagine that you see twelve golden steps in front of you leading away from the blue pool. At the end of the golden steps is a large gold and silver tablet shining with brilliant light. Walk up these twelve golden steps, holding in your heart a knowingness that you will receive a direct indication of your mission in life from what is written on this gold and silver tablet.*

*Slowly climb these twelve steps, observing as much detail about the steps and the radiant scenery about you. Use all of your senses to tune into this landscape. When you reach the tablet, be curious. Look deeply into it.*

*It has your name engraved across it, and underneath the words "My mission in life is..." Look at this golden text, see the light and images on it. Perhaps there is a perfume emanating from these words. Use all of your five senses to explore this tablet, and the writing on it. Touch it, feel it, and hold it. Try to see the words below describing your mission in life. It may just be a knowingness about your mission that you pick up, or you may be able to read every word in detail. After a while allow yourself to fall asleep.*

Practice this technique every night until you begin to get impressions of your mission in life. This could come from dreams, or golden moments during the day. Whatever happens make sure you write it down in your Mission Journal. Some of you will get impressions about qualities of Soul you want to explore as well, so write these down, and any other notes that illustrate deeper insights for you.

## How to Catch Soul's Vision
## Technique 7.

# **Highest Imagination**

This technique is easy for those of you who have a bright imagination. Before we begin this exercise please turn back in your Mission Journal to the place where you did the exercises from the chapter on "Unfolding Your True Greatness". If you remember you noted down all the talents you had, the things people liked about you, and also qualities of Soul that inspired you. Read over your notes of talents and qualities, and ponder on them for a few minutes.

### The Spiritual Exercise

Now close your eyes, taking a few minutes to really relax your body and mind ensuring your entire being is at ease with itself. If your mind is busy from the daily routine take a few moments to balance your thoughts and center yourself. If you feel angry about something, simply decide to agree to feel that way and move on. You can always come back to the anger later. Have your Mission Journal and a pen beside you, and open it to today's page.

*Then in your own time lovingly put your attention at the place between your eyes where your daydreams occur. Now as a love song from the heart of Soul to the divine source, sing this beautiful word HU five times. As you sing HU on each outward breath, imagine the sound uplifting you, taking you to a higher level. And on the fifth*

*HU, imagine you become the golden sparkling heart of Soul, the home of your infinite inspiration.*

*From this high state of consciousness you can see unlimited boundaries. You feel free, as you as Soul, dwell in the stream of divine love. Allow your imagination to ponder on these talents, or qualities you have. Ponder, reflect upon, and wonder at the true greatness of Soul.*

*As you let your imagination roll, allow it to consider what would be a great mission to have in this lifetime, and continue to ponder, wonder and explore it.*

*At some point something will strike the imagination with vitality. You will suddenly come alive in your imagination with an idea, a notion, a direction, a possibility. Follow this through with your imagination, then gently come back from these inner worlds, and in your own time write this impression down. Put in as much detail as possible.*

## Then Each Day

At some time during the day also put your attention on repeating this exercise at a special time. Try to feel excited about it and about the discoveries you will make. Then at that special time repeat the exercise. You can continue from where you left off or start a completely new avenue of inspiration, and when you touch on a line of inspiration come back, and write it down.

At the end of a month or your chosen timeframe you will have a number of inspired impressions of Soul's vision. Perhaps you have a definite impression about a quality of Soul. All you have to do now is select the brightest one of these pictures, impressions or qualities. The one that truly inspires you over the rest.

How to Catch Soul's Vision

Technique 8.

# One Minute Describes Destiny

This is a quick and powerful technique. It works by taking the mind by surprise. The most effective way to do this is to go for a walk somewhere beautiful and peaceful. A place where nature is bountiful and inspiring. Simply walk by the water or amongst the trees, and ponder on the greatness that is within you. Ponder on the talents you have, however great or small they appear. Just spend this quality time with yourself.

## Spiritual Exercise

When you return home find somewhere to contemplate for a few moments. Open your Mission Journal, and have a pen ready. Begin by closing your eyes and relaxing yourself for a few minutes

*Then in your own time lovingly put your attention at the place between your eyes where your daydreams occur. Now as a love song from the heart of Soul to the divine source, sing this beautiful word HU five times. As you sing HU on each outward breath, imagine the sound uplifting you, taking you to a higher level. And on the fifth HU, imagine you become the golden sparkling heart of Soul.*

*In this expanded state of consciousness, allow your imagination to drift back to the beautiful place you have just visited. Allow the natural impressions to flow through, and inspire you, then say to yourself, "If I knew what my mission in life was, what would it be?" Now take a few seconds to come back from these inner worlds, and open your eyes.*

*Within the next sixty seconds write down the answer to your question, "If I knew what my mission in life was, what would it be?" Write down as many things as possible, do not think about it, just do it, ACT AS IF YOU KNOW.*

*Write down what is illuminated in your mind. It may be one thing or six things, just write them all down in your Mission Journal.*

That's all there is to this technique. You will find that what you write down is either an accurate description of Soul's vision or your next step. Many times we need to take these "next steps" to get to the higher ground where we clearly can see our mission in life.

## How to Catch Soul's Vision
## Technique 9.

# <u>Your Turning Points</u>

For this technique I would like you to first review the notes you made from the chapter on "Unfolding Your True Greatness". This technique is best suited for those who are senior in years or those who have had a very rich, and varied experience of life.

Write a heading in your Mission Journal entitled, "Turning Points". Now go back in your mind as far as you can to your childhood days, and write down the first turning point in your life that you remember. Then write down the next turning point in your life, and continue writing down these turning points until you reach today.

A turning point is a major shift in the direction of your life that you, someone else or a situation instigated.

So you should by now, depending on your age, have a long list of turning points in your life. Put a new heading below the turning points called "Learning Points". Now for each turning point, write down what you learned from it, or why you had to make this turning point in your life. Perhaps add what positive lessons you observed or learned. Try and cover every turning point that you remember. Take time to include them all. If you are not clear, then sleep on it, and come back to it the next day when you are fresher.

You will now have a list of turning points, and the lessons that you have learned or the decisions that you had to make at those turning points, and what you learned from them. Now close your Mission Journal and don't write down any more. Take a break from this for at least a week.

## A Week Later

*Sit down, close your eyes and relax. Then in your own time lovingly put your attention at the place between your eyes where your daydreams occur. Now as a love song from the heart of Soul to the divine source, sing this beautiful word HU five times. As you sing HU on each outward breath, imagine the sound uplifting you, taking you to a higher level. And on the fifth HU, imagine you become the golden sparkling heart of Soul.*

*After singing the HU silently absorb the inner radiance of Soul for a while before gently returning from this inner dimension. As you open your eyes ask yourself, "If I knew what my mission in life was, what would it be?" Next open your Mission Journal and begin to review the list of turning and learning points you last wrote there.*

Start at the beginning and work your way through. When you reach the last one look back and ask yourself if there is a pattern of learning, or maybe a pattern of turning points. You may be able to see a direction that your life is going in from these changes which have been occurring throughout your life. Write down your impressions of these changes and what you think Soul has been trying to do or show you by orchestrating these events in your life.

## Then

Ask yourself what would be the next step or next turning point if these continued in the same pattern? Where do you think these turning points are leading you? How do they describe your mission in life? How have these turning points equipped you for a mission in life? What would that mission in life be? What qualities of Soul are most illuminated for you, or most used during your experiences?

Ask as many questions and write down as many answers as you can to the questions that you ask.

## And While You Sleep

Also take these questions into sleep. Ask them to yourself before you fall asleep. When you awake write down in as much detail the impressions and answers you get. This method, like the others, works on the principle that you have been in training for your mission in life from the moment you were born.

## And Finally

Review your notes, and experiences to see the vision Soul is illustrating.

How to Catch Soul's Vision

Technique 10.

# **Letters From the Ocean**

I would like you to find somewhere to relax and be still for thirty minutes or so. Close your eyes and focus on the quietness within.

### *Spiritual Exercise*

*Then in your own time lovingly put your attention at the place between your eyes where your daydreams occur. Now as a love song from the heart of Soul to the divine source, sing this beautiful word HU five times. As you sing HU on each outward breath, imagine the sound uplifting you, taking you to a higher level. And on the fifth HU, imagine you become the golden sparkling heart of Soul. Then continue to sing the HU silently.*

*Imagine that as you sing this sound of Soul you are transported in your Soul body to the edge of a majestic ocean, somewhere in the higher worlds of light and sound. You stand on the edge of this mighty ocean. You feel as one with this ocean. You feel its power as the waves thunder onto the beach. You are also its beauty as you see the brilliant sun dancing on the surface to shower you with a million points of light, as you also are the light.*

*As you look out across these waters ask yourself the question "If I knew what my mission in life was, what would it be?" Then expect an answer.*

*As you continue to look out towards this ocean bathed in the divine love of God you see a letter coming out of the sparkling sea towards you. With each wave it floats ever closer until it is washed up at your feet. The letter has on it the words "My mission in life: (followed by your name)". Try to feel excitement and curiosity as you pick up this letter and open it.*

*As you read it you recognize your hand writing and the words; "My mission in life is ..................." Then in your own time gently come back from these inner worlds and open your eyes.*

For some, your mission will be clearly written in the letter. So write this down in your Mission Journal. If you have not seen a clear description of your mission from the letter then try again tomorrow. Do this for up to a month. One day the words will appear clearly. In the meantime just know that you are constantly moving closer to discovering this vision. It is all about clearing the channel between the mind and Soul.

How to Catch Soul's Vision

Technique 11.

# **<u>Beautiful Pictures</u>**
# **<u>of Destiny</u>**

This is a very practical and visual method. You will need to collect or buy a large number of magazines. Try to make the topics of the magazines as varied as possible. The only other requirement is that these magazines have lots of pictures in them. I would also suggest that as you collect these magazines try to include ones that you would normally buy as well as ones that you would never buy, and some that you may occasionally buy.

Now cut out at least sixty pictures from these magazines. I usually paste them onto a piece of cardboard, and cut it to the shape of each picture. It makes them more durable, in case you want to do this exercise more than once. After you have cut these pictures out, wait a week before looking at them again, just to clear the mind of the images.

### <u>One Week Later</u>

Sort through these pictures and pick out the ones that inspire you. Place these in a separate group.

### <u>*Spiritual Exercise*</u>

*Sit comfortably. Close your eyes and relax, putting your attention gently on the stillnes within. Then in your own time lovingly put your attention at the place between your eyes where your daydreams occur. Now as a love song from the heart of Soul to the divine source, sing this beautiful word HU five times. As you sing HU on each outward breath, imagine the sound uplifting you, taking you to a higher level. And on the fifth HU, imagine you become the golden sparkling heart of Soul. Then continue to sing HU silently for a few more moments.*

Gently bring your attention back to the present and feel this divine love pouring through your life as you open your eyes. Spend up to twenty minutes on this exercise.

In front of you are the pictures you just selected. They, in some way, mean something to you. Open your Mission Journal, hold each picture in turn, and write down what it is that inspires you about this picture. Use Soul's infinite viewpoint to look at all perspectives.

Ask yourself, "Is there something represented by this picture that I can do that serves life? What qualities of Soul does this picture illuminate in me? What is there in this picture that uplifts life for others and myself?"

Continue to ponder on this. It does not matter how far out or how unconnected your ideas may be, write them down. As you write, continue to let the imagination explore possibilities so that one idea may trigger several different possibilities. At the end of this exercise you will have a list of things that inspire your life.

### The Picture

Now try to form these notes into a picture of Soul's vision. Look for the connections between the notes you have written. You will end up with a description of Soul's vision that is most inspiring.

## How to Catch Soul's Vision
## Technique 12.

# <u>Look Back in Love</u>

For this technique to work you need to really use the full breath of your imagination. So make yourself comfortable, close your eyes and gently relax your mind and body.

### <u>Spiritual Exercise</u>

*Then in your own time lovingly put your attention at the place between your eyes where your daydreams occur. Now as a love song from the heart of Soul to the divine source, sing this beautiful word HU five times. As you sing HU on each outward breath, imagine the sound uplifting you, taking you to a higher level. And on the fifth HU, imagine you become the golden sparkling heart of Soul. Then continue to sing the HU silently.*

*As you sing this sound, imagine that you are in the future. You have lived a fantastic life here on earth and ahead of you is another fantastic journey. However you pause to reflect on this life on earth. You observe your successes, triumphs, skills learned, and your fulfilled completed mission here on earth.*

*Feel a great sense of love and jubilation tumble through your body as you reflect on a great life. As you continue to ponder on this fantastic life you come across this moment in time today, where you changed the course of your life for the better. Look at the decision you made, and how it changed the outcome of your life. Then roll forward to the end of this lifetime, and ask yourself the question, "What has been my mission in life, a mission so unique and fabulous that has released so many great talents within myself? What has my mission in life been?"*

*You can also ask, "What qualities of Soul have I been working with to fulfill my mission in life?" Then gently return from this inner dimension and when you are ready, open your eyes.*

Now write down all your impressions including the qualities of Soul you feel you have used to fulfill your mission in life. If you have a clear picture of your mission in life then write this down in as much detail as possible. Otherwise write down the impressions from Soul's high viewpoint.

# Chapter 5.

# From Vision to Mission

## Changing the Vision Into an Effective and Inspiring Mission

This chapter, and the previous one are especially interlinked. You may find it necesary to shuttle between these two until you have a clear mission defined or your next step outlined.

We are going to deal with the essential matter of how to turn the vision into a crystal clear mission, filled with vitality and purpose. The first thing to do is review the journey so far. To do this I suggest you go to the start of your Mission Journal and review all your notes and experiences up to your last entries where you caught the vision.

Now take a break for about a month or so. This is necessary so that your consciousness can breathe and balance itself out to the new levels of expanded awareness that you have been experiencing. During your rest period it is a good idea to continue doing a daily HU song spiritual exercise, lasting between ten to twenty minutes.

## One Month Later

Okay, let's start by looking at some examples of the visions some people have caught...

> *"After using the "One Minute Describes Destiny" technique, I found myself writing down a goal I have had a for a long time. It was to move from the busy city and live in the countryside. I have always been worried by what others might think and I have always done what has been expected of me, but now I know I must and will move, and I am going to set the process in motion immediately. I don't exactly know what the future holds for me. This technique has made me feel so strong about what I know I need to do. I am sure I will be stronger as a result of doing it, which can only be good."*
> *P. Davis London, England.*

> *"I was driving in my car one day, several weeks after reading the chapter, "Unfolding Your True Greatness". I have since then, been producing a long list of positive things that I can do. Anyway I*

*was out driving one sunny day when I suddenly realized that I would make a really good relationships counsellor. Wow! It had suddenly dawned on me how people came to me when in trouble, and I was always able to make them feel happy, and leave with a positive direction. I guess that I have never really valued this. I have just done it. Maybe I can go into business with this."*

K. Stevens  Surrey, England

*"This is amazing. I have been using the dream method, giving myself positive instructions about knowing my mission when I wake up, and it happened last night. This is fantastic. I am so happy. I saw it all. Obviously I don't want to tell all yet, but I saw myself in the future doing something which I know I would love. I have no skills in that area right now, but I can learn. I am so excited."*

A. Edwards  Minneapolis, U.S.A.

## When It Comes From the Heart of Soul

**It is absolutely essential that your vision comes from Soul.** However, because of the way the human consciousness works, it may appear to be from Soul, but its source may be from a much lower level of consciousness. The result is that the vision will not stay the course, it will evaporate like water in a hot desert.

Anything that we create that really makes a positive difference for the better begins in the heart of Soul.

There are always very clear indicators as to where your vision has come from. All you have to do is ask yourself

- 123 -

these questions about the vision, and I suggest that you write them down in your Mission Journal...

- *Do I feel very strongly about it?*
- *Am I absolutely adamant this is it?*
- *Does it feel heavy?*
- *Does it feel right ?*
- *Do I intuitively sense it is right?*
- *Is the vision deeply inspiring?*
- *Am I filled with enthusiasm?*
- *Am I still pondering on what I see?*
- *Have I a gentle knowingness?*
- *Does it fill me with love?*
- *Am I inspired by the vision and still pondering on the possibilities?*
- *Can I see Soul's vision clearly?*

If you have answered yes to any of the questions numbered one through three, then there is still a higher expression of Soul's vision to bring through. However, if you have answered yes to one of the remaining questions, then you are either on the shores of catching the vision or you have caught the heart of Soul's vision.

If Soul's vision is not clear enough you have some choices. Either continue with this chapter which may help to focus the vision a bit better or return to the previous chapter and maybe choose a different method to catch the vision.

From Soul's viewpoint everything is seen as an infinite divine expression of love, so it continues to ponder on the vision. It is never adamant about anything. It is always expanding, encompassing and growing in wisdom and love. Soul is like an endless river that keeps on getting wider and deeper. The further it flows, the more it knows; the more it knows, the more it sees; the more it sees, the more it loves and so on.

## The Law of Silence

Once we have either experienced Soul's vision or directly perceived our mission, we must obey the Law of Silence, or we may lose the whole thing. When a vision or mission comes from Soul we become a channel for an infinite amount of divine love. This beautiful and inspiring divine love constantly pours through us seeking outer manifestation as we cannot hold onto it. So share love with others, but don't share the reasons for it as it is very personal and special.

Many people find it extremely hard to stay silent simply because the ego has suffered a bypass operation, and will find any way possible to play an active role again. Telling a friend what we are going to do is the top choice for the ego. So many people soon lose these exalted states of consciousness once they have discovered Soul's vision. They chat to everyone who seems remotely interested. The more we talk about what we are going to do, the better we tend to feel because the energy is coming straight from the heart of Soul, and it swamps the Astral body with enthusiasm.

Eventually this energy gets cut off as the ego gets in the way trying to take credit. So some time during this period of chit chat which could be days, weeks or months, a feeling of depression usually fills our being as we suddenly realize that we have not really moved on with the vision. This is followed by having to justify to others why we are "Just all talk and no action." We have all met these people who just talk about things they are going to do, and never get there.

## Choose Your Mission Helpers Carefully

It may be that we need other people to be involved in what we are doing, but we should never tell them the whole picture (this is ours, and ours alone). Only tell people who can help, and make sure that they are trustworthy, and don't chatter to others which will leak the energy out as well. Just because someone is a friend does not automatically mean that they can help, however well intentioned they may be. I recall an incident when I was a child which went like this...

*My eldest brother was really into model railways. At the time, he had been collecting model trains for many years, and he bought this large sheet of wood about the size of a large dining table. He set up this enormous working railway system with stations and landscaped it with fields and trees. It really looked good. As a nine year old child I was really impressed. One day, while my mom was at work, I stayed at home with my two brothers, and my eldest decided to bring his model railway down from his bedroom, to demonstrate it to my brother and me. Well he was all set up and because this sheet of chipboard was too large for our dining table, he had to support half of it on the back of a chair. The hours went by, and he then invited me to operate one of the steam trains. I sat on the supporting chair, and went to change a signal, but I could not reach it. In my wisdom I moved the chair so I could reach, and the whole model railway on this sheet of wood pivoted for a brief second on the corner of the table, then slid to the ground smashing up everything. It was a mess! My eldest brother was beyond furious, and attacked me both verbally and physically as I cowered into a corner of the room. For the next two hours I watched my brother picking up, and gluing back the pieces of his dream I had destroyed. Finally I was rescued when my mom came home.*

This is an example of someone (me) being well intentioned trying to help but not really understanding or having enough common sense to deliver the help where it is best needed. Being well intentioned simply isn't good enough. Someone with wisdom, knowledge, and experience in life will serve us much better than blind enthusiasm. Whenever I meet someone who may be able to help <u>I always ask them silently on the inner</u>; (i.e. Soul to Soul) "Can you help me in my mission or can we help each other in life?" I then watch to see how the conversation or situation develops. It usually works because **only truth flows from Soul to Soul.**

I just want to briefly touch on networking with people (not computers). This is very important. Whenever you meet someone of interest take to time to explore and understand what their talents in life are, what their experiences are, and if you have anything in common. Always if possible take down a telephone number, and give them a business card. This might sound very cold to some people, but it is a great way to get to know people at a deeper level as well, which might never have occurred. If networking is new to you then I suggest you read up about it. There are a number of books on the topic, but essentially it is a way to increase the opportunities of success simply because you are now connecting to many more people. I often get a call from someone who was given my name by someone else who was given my name by someone else...... who says that they want to talk about a new project. They are interested in what I do, and I may benefit from what they do.

Networking really does work, and it really helps the "little people" like you and me. Consider this, someone four thousand miles away on the other side of the world could have been given your name by a colleague, and be discussing some business that could change your life forever for the best. Anyway back to the vision...

## How to Empower the Vision

We are going to look at how to empower and enliven the vision with the abundant love and vitality of Soul. It is a simple spiritual exercise that will take about thirty minutes of your time each day. So first read this through a few times to become comfortable with what you have to do.

1. *Find your special place where you won't be disturbed. Sit down and relax completely. Imagine that each outward breath you take exhales some tension and each inward breath infuses calm and peacefulness to your being.*

2. *Next, I would suggest that you sing this spiritual word HU for about five minutes. As before, sing the HU from the heart of Soul as a love song to God. Afterwards gently ponder for a few moments on the positive difference your mission is going to make in life.*

3. *Now we are going to increase the vitality of the vision, so first of all in your imagination put yourself in the middle of your vision. See yourself there as clearly as possible, looking out and about from your center. If you have the awareness you can also be the observer as well. Now increase the brightness of the colors you see and dwell on this for a few minutes, then increase the clarity of what you see. Get a real sharp focus on points of detail. If there are sounds to be heard,*

increase the volume so it is very loud. Then the fragrances; if there are none, put some in, and make them very strong. This applies to taste as well. Finally touch things, and increase their texture so they feel three dimensional. What you are doing is involving your senses which have a very high expression in Soul. Getting your senses involved allows much more vitality to roll through your vision. Do this for about fifteen minutes.

4. Lastly fill the vision you see with bright boundless love, in other words **"love it into life"**. As Soul you are filled infinitely with love, so see this love pouring from your heart into the vision. **See this love giving life itself to the vision.** Spend time pouring love into the vision. Nothing is ever lost and it will come back to you a thousandfold. **Love is the greatest motivator of any human action.** It will create a three dimensional vision and empower it beyond measure.

5. Now take your time to gently come back from this inner vision and open your eyes.

## Alternatively...

If you have trouble with this imagination technique then try describing the vision you have on paper. Do the above Steps One through Five, but write down and express in words how the vision is empowered; what you see, what you feel, etc.

## Serving Life Makes a Big Difference

Each and every Soul on this earth is here to learn that they are Soul. Ultimately we will become co-workers with the divine source, call it God or whatever name you wish to ascribe. Becoming a co-worker with this divine source is all about serving life, and your mission is part of this. **If your mission in life serves life then it will stand a one hundred percent greater chance of working out.**

It is a good idea to check how your mission will serve life. It may be that you have not correctly perceived it as yet, it may well be coming from Soul, but your interpretation is slightly off beat.

So ask yourself the following questions:

1. *How does it serve life?*

2. *How will it make a difference for the better for me?*

3. *How will it make a difference for the better for others?*

4. *How will it make a difference for the better in this world?*

**If the mission serves life then you will find that the entire spiritual universe aligns itself behind you when you act. You will notice time and time again divine moments where it seems that everything in life is behind you.** This is because your mission is a gift to life, and Divine Spirit works closely with you, and through you to help you achieve your aims.

## Making a Difference for the Better

I have used the words making a difference for the better, and to me that means looking at what is currently the situation, or what is provided, or what currently happens or how things currently work. Then I look at the expectations I have, or the expectations other people have, or even the expectations nature might have, depending on what it is I am going to do. Then I simply evaluate the difference, and try to fill the gap. There will always be a gap because the consciousness of the human race is always unfolding. **If you do something that falls short of filling the gap, it will succeed, but success will be short lived as you will be catching the tail end of people's expectations.**

**If you do something that fills the gap exactly it will be a great success almost every time.**

Take for example the umbrella. The creator matched people's expectations exactly, and its longevity is living proof.

**However if you overstretch the gap then it will take much longer to become successful as it will only be understood by a few, and you will have to wait for the consciousness of people to expand enough to accept it.** This is the problem that befalls a lot of scientific inventors.

So whatever you do, try and measure the difference it is going to make, and ask yourself if it fits exactly, or falls short or overstretches the gap. It may be that you want to do something that falls short or overstretches the mark, and that is fine too.

## Goals to Clarify the Mission

The only difference between a vision and a mission is the lowest plane of existence from where you observe the action. At the Soul level Soul's vision is Soul's mission.

On the Mental level, the mind expresses and carries out the vision in its own way. This works all the way down to the Physical level where you are waiting to effect this vision as a mission in the physical world. To turn the vision into a mission you need to identify a set of goals that best describe and represent the vision on the Physical Plane. This means that you will have a series of goals that can be short, medium, and long term and when taken as a whole group they accurately express Soul's vision.

## Techniques to Bring Out the Mission

I suggest that you give yourself at least a month to do this. I have outlined the best methods I know for achieving this. You can adapt them to fit your style of doing things.

### First Method of Two (Read both methods first.)

This is the method of free association, or connecting diamonds as I like to call it. Basically, write the vision down on a blank page of your Mission Journal. Then write down the very first thought you have that could be a goal connected to the vision. Continue to ponder on what you have just written for a moment, then write down the next "connected idea" to the last you wrote down. Ponder and write down what idea is connected to the last one you wrote, and so on.

The key is never to mentalize on what you are going to write, just write it down. That way it flows from Soul. If one particular line of thought fails to really get anywhere, that is it does not flow, then stop. Start another stream of ideas or pondering from the vision in the center or top of the page, and produce another stream of pondering. So you will end up with a page like this...

*This is Anne's example. Her vision is of painting flowers; Soul's qualities of simplicity, truth and beauty really inspired her also...*

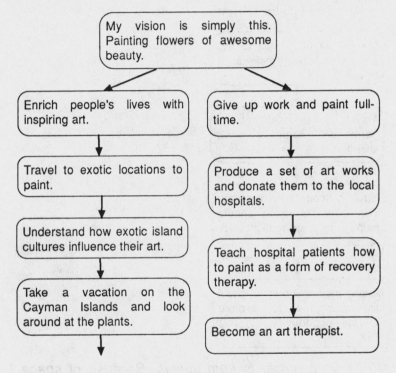

Continued on next page

Study a degree at the island's local college on native art.

Maybe set up a business to export my art to Europe or America.

Maybe set up a stall to sell the art to holiday makers on the island.

Maybe even set up a permanent home on this island.

Have to look at immigration. The work I'm doing should help my application for residency.

Making my home on this island will allow me to explore different opportunities in this area.

*The next example is from James. Because of space I have only shown two of the idea streams. From the exercises he knows that he is going to invent something. Soul's quality of creativity seems to always be illuminated with any exercise that he does, and he has an image of creating something that makes a difference to the way people in general use herbs.*

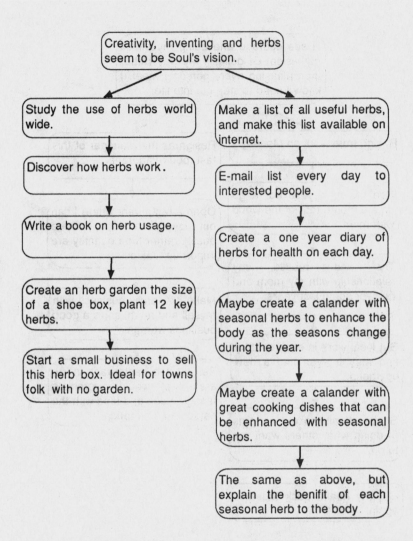

Creativity, inventing and herbs seem to be Soul's vision.

Study the use of herbs world wide.

Discover how herbs work.

Write a book on herb usage.

Create an herb garden the size of a shoe box, plant 12 key herbs.

Start a small business to sell this herb box. Ideal for towns folk with no garden.

Make a list of all useful herbs, and make this list available on internet.

E-mail list every day to interested people.

Create a one year diary of herbs for health on each day.

Maybe create a calander with seasonal herbs to enhance the body as the seasons change during the year.

Maybe create a calander with great cooking dishes that can be enhanced with seasonal herbs.

The same as above, but explain the benifit of each seasonal herb to the body.

*In the following final example of turning the vision into a mission we see how Julie has received her next step. It is not the full mission, but she knows that she must take her next step to be able to move on to greater things.*

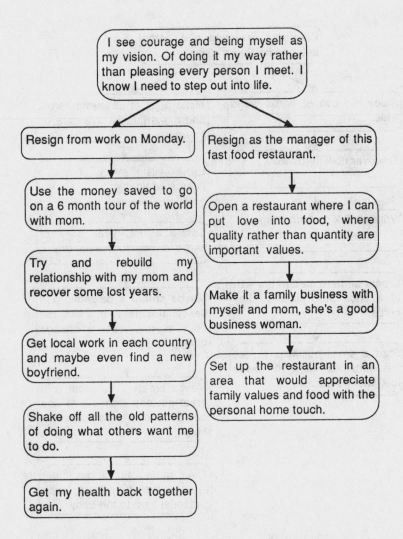

I see courage and being myself as my vision. Of doing it my way rather than pleasing every person I meet. I know I need to step out into life.

Resign from work on Monday.

Resign as the manager of this fast food restaurant.

Use the money saved to go on a 6 month tour of the world with mom.

Open a restaurant where I can put love into food, where quality rather than quantity are important values.

Try and rebuild my relationship with my mom and recover some lost years.

Make it a family business with myself and mom, she's a good business woman.

Get local work in each country and maybe even find a new boyfriend.

Set up the restaurant in an area that would appreciate family values and food with the personal home touch.

Shake off all the old patterns of doing what others want me to do.

Get my health back together again.

As you can see, what each person originally saw of their vision was limited by their experience. Freeing themselves to ponder and wonder through various possibilities allowed the mind to have a greater experience and measure of Soul's vision. In these cases

I have only shown two threads of ideas, but there were at least fifteen different threads. Each different, but all emanating from the same central vision. This process of connecting diamonds really does bring the vision into the physical. Some of the steps will be specific events that may be so awe inspiring that you just have to stop, and take it in. I suggest that you follow as many threads as possible so that you can acknowledge to yourself that you have explored as fully as possible the scope of the vision.

**At the end of the process put a "√" beside each event from any of the streams that truly illuminate and inspire you**. Then I suggest that you sleep on it, and in the morning look again at the events you have marked. Ask yourself which one is the brightest then follow this one. If more than one is illuminated for you, pick the one you wish to do the most. Keep the others, and make notes in your journal about the one you have chosen, and the ones remaining. Now ask yourself the following key questions:

1. *Will I love doing this?*
2. *Does it serve life?*
3. *How does it make a difference for the better?*

**If you can answer positively to these three questions and you still feel illuminated and inspired then you have truly discovered your next mission in life.** Write this down and we can go forward. However, if you cannot answer positively to these then look back on the other events or goals you marked with a "√", and ask the same three key questions again. If you still have no success, go back to the previous stage of connecting diamonds, and either create a new stream of possibilities or review one of the streams you ignored. See what, if anything, inspires you here. Follow the process through until you have a mission that serves yourself, and life, and truly makes a difference for the better.

## Second Method (Read both methods first.)

This method for finding the mission is a lot shorter than the previous, and a lot simpler, and suits those who can see the truth easily. So here is method two...

*Select a particular day of the week ahead of where you are now. This is the day where you will identify a group of ideas or goals that characterize the vision. So from now on, and until the appointed day, ponder with great expectation on discovering your mission, on how you could best express Soul's vision. Ponder upon how you would like to express this vision, particularly what activities would be exciting, and interesting to do. What activities would make a difference for the better in life. On the appointed day write down what you pull through as goals or aims. It does not matter how many ideas or goals you identify just write them down in your Mission Journal. Then when this is complete put the activity aside for a few days, and rest up from it.*

*When you return to this task, highlight the ideas or goals you have listed that truly illuminate for you, the ones that inspire your heart to open, the ones you can see yourself doing. Now from this smaller group pick out the activity or goal that is most exciting, the one that has that special something in it. If you still cannot decide, draw up a list of the advantages and disadvantages for each idea or goal.*

*Consider and note down the plus points and the minus points for each. Then take the one with the most advantages and ask youself these key questions:*

*1. Will I love doing this?*
*2. Does it serve life?*
*3. How does it make a difference for the better?*

**If you still feel illuminated and inspired about it then you have truly discovered your next mission in life.**

## Review and Focus on Each Goal

Whichever method you choose, it is important to review each of the goals you have identified and make sure that they fulfill some basic characteristics. I have listed these below. If your goals don't measure up to these characteristics then I suggest that you review them, and redefine them.

**1. They are crystal clear.**
**2. They must be realistic for you.**
**3. They hold a quality of Soul.**

## Plan Each Event

Next you need to plan and organize when you want these goals to occur. The simple way to do this is to write down each goal in the order you require it to happen, and then add a note to explain why this order is important. The timing of each goal or event is critical to the success of it. The best way I know to resolve the timing issue is to initially set the goal and a date by which you reasonably think you can achieve it.

Look at the resources you need to achieve it. This could be material, money, time, effort, etc. If necessary adjust the date so that your resources will be there on time.

Lastly, in your imagination, put yourself forward in time to when you wish to achieve your goal. Then look back to now, and ask yourself, "Did I give myself enough time?" If the answer is no, move the goal forward in time, and repeat the exercise until all your goals can be met given the amount of time and resources you have or can acquire.

Planning each event you see is important. Each goal is a stimulus for great success in itself. **When you plan an event you focus the awesome spiritual current flowing from Soul to a pinpoint in time.** This allows your entire being to begin working towards that goal. Each significant step you plan succeeds better than the unplanned step. Each sequence of actions you plan runs together better than the unplanned ones. Planning works on the Mental Plane, and disciplines the mind which is critical to your success in whatever you do in life.

## Does it Fit?

Ask yourself if the set of goals which are now set somewhere in time, match and fulfill your mission in life. Is this the best representation of the original vision you had? If the answer is no, then go back, and discover where the goals or planning can be improved.

I just wanted to mention at this point that it is unwise to set goals that others are unwilling participants in. This means try not to set goals that involve other people doing something that you will later come to depend on unless they have freely agreed to achieve this goal with you. So setting a goal to travel the world with Mary in twelve months time is unwise if she currently has no interest in travelling with you.

## How to Quicken the Goals

At this point you should have a clear set of goals written down that clearly define the vision of Soul and a plan of action. I would like to suggest a method to quicken these goals, and make them even more real than before.

Take each goal you have written down. Think about and write down an event you expect to occur just before the goal happens, and an event that occurs just after the goal is achieved. Here is an example...

*The main goal is to move to a new country, and live. The "just before" event might be the thrill of getting on the airplane or maybe the thrill of flying over the destination airport before landing.*

*The "just after" event could be your first night in this new country, and you find yourself without any electricity to cook with. Or the sense of relief and thrill as you hug your new partner, or maybe the thrill of opening the curtains on the first new day in this new country and watching the sunrise.*

As you can see, these surrounding events really encapsulate and empower the original goal, giving it more life, validity and vitality than before. The overall method for bringing this mission into reality is to spend ten minutes, three times a day seeing in your imagination the mission. You need to pick the time of the day that best suits you. Most people prefer the morning, noon and evening times. All you need to do then is see the before, the during, and the after event, and with each of these three events fill them with enthusiasm, excitement and boundless love.

## Staying in Balance

There are three stages that you may go through once you have caught your vision, and the clearer the vision or mission you identify, the greater these effects can be. You really need to be mindful of these so that you can stay in balance. For example...

*You wake up one morning, and to your surprise you have seen Soul's vision during dream time or maybe you have clearly identified a set of goals that accurately defines a mission for you...you feel inspired. This is truly a golden day for you, and over the next few weeks and months you can become ...*

### The Busy Fool
You find yourself getting busy on everything! Anything that comes along that seems remotely connected to the vision or mission, you're into it. You are grabbing at every bubble on the surface of the water. You are very excited and excitable. You also find it difficult to keep your mouth shut at this stage.

*Well, time passes, and you have grabbed at anything and everything. The excitement begins to subside and you can become.....*

### The Motivated Idiot
You now become all action, with no vision. All the busy activity of the previous stage has made you lose focus on the all important vision, but you are still pumped with

energy. You feel motivated. You are like the person who is all dressed up with nowhere to go.

*Eventually calm reigns. You begin to come to your senses, and after spending some time re-aligning to your original vision you become once more...*

## Balanced and Clear
You begin to see how you are going to implement your mission. You begin to take measured action in a controlled way and move forward in a positive direction. Motivated, balanced and focused.

The phases I have called the Busy Fool, and the Motivated Idiot can last for several years in the worst cases I have come across. I myself was also lost in these stages for about two years. **The reason I and other people became lost in this wilderness of false hope was because there was no plan to take the highly charged vision and convert it into a mission.** This next section covers these vital steps of creating actions that convert the vision into a mission.

## <u>Vital Steps</u>

1. In your Mission Journal describe the goals that now define the vision. Write them on a yellow card, then place this yellow card in your house or office where you can see it. If others can see it make sure that the words on the card will not tell them what you are going to do. So twist the words in some way to disguise the meaning to others.

2. Constantly review your plan of action. Ask yourself the question, "Am I going in the right direction and am I happy with this direction?"

3. In the morning, at midday and before you go to sleep spend a few minutes of quiet time with your mission. I suggest that you allow your imagination to lift you into your wonderful destiny. See and feel the reality of your mission. Sense the fragrances, the textures, the objects therein and the colors. Use all of your five senses to explore the reality of your mission. Become enthused, consumed and inspired with the detail in the image. Allow enthusiasm to flow into every aspect of your imagination. And do this in the sequence of the before, during and after as previously described.

4. Constantly ask yourself questions like...

   *How can I bring this mission into reality?*
   *What is the next best step to take?*
   *Am I taking the right action?*

5. Never get fixed into thinking that there is only one way to do something. Remember as Soul you have an infinite viewpoint on life, so use this perspective as much as possible.

6. There is NO rush. Take your time, measure your actions, control your efforts and keep focused on the vision of your mission. Keep it alive in your imagination, everyday.

7. Take some direct action that is related to your mission everyday. Always honor and acknowledge each step you take.

## Vital Mission Reports

It is very important to produce a monthly Mission Report. I have outlined a simple framework below that can be put into the Mission Journal. Then each month run through the ten point checklist and fill in your comments under each month. Always review the previous month's report before filling in the current month. After a few months you will be able to see trends and gain inspiration to help you to fulfill your mission.

| TASK | JAN | FEB |
|---|---|---|
| Declare your mission here every month. | | |
| Is my direction in tune with my mission? | | |
| What lessons in life am I learning? | | |
| What spiritual principles have I discovered? | | |
| What stumbling blocks have I come across? | | |
| What new opportunities have I discovered? | | |
| What am I truly grateful for this month? | | |
| What successes have I experienced? | | |
| What new thing have I discovered about my mission? | | |
| Did anything open and fill my heart with love? | | |

## Personal Missions

There are a number of people who have said to me that they can only see a personal mission ahead for themselves. These personal missions have included mountain climbing, hiking around parts of China, going on underwater expeditions, parachuting, learning to fly airplanes, etc. Well that is fine, and I always encourage them. They might not be able to see how it makes a difference for the better, or how it serves life, but that is fine too. For these people the experience will make them stronger in heart and more courageous. They are facing challenges that will test the skill, draw on their hidden talents and allow the true qualities of Soul to shine through. They will return home different people from when they left, able to give to life more than before. This may be part of their mission.

In conclusion, I would urge you to be patient, work through this chapter at your own pace. A wise friend of mine once said to me, "Andrew, be patient. **Do a small thing everyday towards your mission and you will succeed.** It is from you doing the small things that big things will happen."

A guide point to note is that when your consciousness begins to align with the direction you are moving in, you will begin to see reflections of your consciousness in everyday life. That is to say, if you want to buy a red car, you will begin to see examples of red cars of the same make all about you; on television, parked beside you, a picture of one in the newspaper etc. It is but a sign post that you are on the right road.

# Chapter 6.
# The Loving Wisdom of Soul

## How to Touch the Highest Levels of Wisdom Available to Us on a Daily Basis.

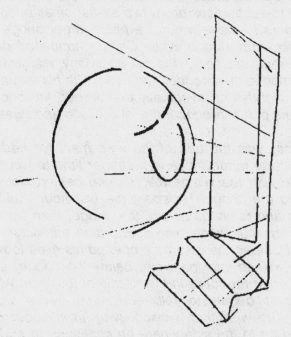

Talking about wisdom and sounding wise is one thing, but to me what counts is **being able to flow the deep wisdom of Soul into our daily life.** So we are going to specifically deal with developing practical daily wisdom. I recall from my old Kung Fu instructor this story...

A long time ago in a small Chinese village there lived two men. One was a champion strong man, the other a small wise old man. The champion strong man issued a challenge to the wise old man in order to gain the respect of the village folk who revered the wise old man. The young strong man could never understand why. He had never seen this wise old man do anything while he lifted heavy weights, and did death defying feats in the village square every week.

Eventually the wise old man accepted the challenge which was to each knock down two similar small bridges made of rocks to make way for a much larger bridge to serve an expanded community. On the appointed day, the strong man set about the bridge. Many village folk came to watch as he pounded the rocks with his feet and hands. By nightfall he eventually demolished the bridge to the cheers of the village, and a lot of blood and sweat.

The next day was the turn of the wise man. He had to knock down the other bridge in a shorter time to win the contest. So with the village folk walking behind him he approached the bridge. He spent the first hour walking backwards and forwards across the bridge, then he sat down in deep meditation. The strong man felt victory in his grasp, but then the wise man opened his eyes took a long stick, walked into the water below the bridge, and began to nudge the rocks in the middle of the arch. After a while dust began to fall, and small rocks were dislodged. The wise man walked away from under the bridge, and off to the side where he continued to nudge the rocks. Then with a creaking and snapping the bridge slowly began to crumble. He had taken a fifth of the time the strong man had taken.

This is an example of how being wise and taking wise action gets us through life the easy way. Wisdom is one of the highest qualities of Soul, **but you need courage to be wise**. Being wise usually means doing it your way, against the herding instinct of many people.

We live in a world that is dominated by knowledge. People believe in it, live by it, and even die by it. Sadly, it has become too important. Knowledge dominates the lower worlds below the Soul Plane. Conversely wisdom is the driving force behind truth in the higher worlds. This is not to discount knowledge, it is a quality of Soul, and knowledge is the all important step before wisdom. Yet of all these, it is divine love that will ignite and illuminate the divine wisdom of Soul.

Today, there is much emphasis placed on academic qualifications being minimum thresholds to gaining particular employment. While in the most part this academic knowledge is very important, it is not everything. A person's ability to solve a problem comes in some part from their knowledge, but in the most part it is determined by whether a person loves the job or not. If they love what they do the problem will be easily solved. If they are not inspired the problem will take a long time to be resolved.

The reason for this is that common knowledge must first be applied and exhausted before divine inspiration begins to really flow. Without a love for the task at hand, the common knowledge appears like an endless lead weight around the neck. Love allows the mind to race through the common knowledge thus allowing the wisdom of Soul to flow into the situation, and solve it.

Living your mission in life will allow you to touch the loving wisdom of Soul. This is the smart way to live life. It means acting from the highest possible state of consciousness that your human form can sustain. Many people confuse knowledge and wisdom. Wisdom is a living energy flowing from the heart of Soul, and it unfolds when you begin to take action. **The more wisdom that flows through you the more wisdom you are able to absorb. So you become wiser and it becomes simpler to tap into those exalted states of consciousness.**

Wisdom works from an attitude of great humility, and you may well find yourself doing and saying things that are deeply profound. At the same time you will be able to observe the ego trying to draw particular actions or words you say to the attention of others. This needs to be kept in check. Doing or saying things because you know others will say "WOW" is how you start a following. Soon you will have people praising you and sending in donations. This is certainly one way to slow down your spiritual evolution.

The true power of wisdom is acting as if you already know the answer, because in the heart of Soul you already do. This is risky when done from the mind, but it flows so well when done from Soul. Our lower bodies are like children who take advice from parents. We need the experiences of life to learn the deep truth buried within each exerience.

## Solving Problems

So when you have a problem, lovingly **act as if** you know the answer, and develop a love for "having the problem solved". Or put another way **allow the problem to**

**inspire you** rather then depress and worry you. This gives Soul the space to breathe its wisdom into the problem so we approach each problem from a new perspective of...

> *I know that I can.....*
> *I have the answer.....*
> *I can do that.....*
> *I see the way through.....*
> *I know the way...*

The other way to get an answer from Soul is to ask the right question, as in these examples...

> *How can I do this?*
> *What is the answer to this?*
> *What do I have to learn to proceed?*
> *What is my next step?*

Asking, "Why, why, why did this happen?" is an emotional reaction, and never goes higher than that, so any answers that come will be emotive or reactive. Whereas, "How can I...?" is about taking action, using the wisdom of Soul to solve the problem. There is a saying that goes like this...

> *God will not do for you what you*
> *must first do for yourself.*

Too often some people sit back and expect others to do for them what they must do for themselves. Or they complain when things are not right rather then set about using their wisdom and talents to fix the problem.

I knew a friend a long time ago who wanted a job so he prayed for the perfect one. The months went by, and he never got the job he was dreaming about. He believed that God was going to get it for him. He spent years of his life praying for employment, while most of his friends were in their second job. It never occurred to him that he must look in the paper or take some kind of direct action himself. Somehow, this was not spiritual enough for him. So he continued to pray. The last I heard of him he was still on unemployment, and still praying for that perfect job. There are really no free rides in life, whether we are spiritual or not. **Being spiritual is about living from the heart of Soul in the heart of this physical life.**

## Universal Wisdom of All Souls

If you are in a dilemma, and need another viewpoint, and you have no one to ask, then try using your imagination.

Choose someone whose views you respect, and ask them what they would do in your dilemma. It is as simple as that. Let's take a situation where you are struggling to decide whether to move to another country to pursue one of your goals or stay where you are. Both seem equally good and are valid options. All you need to do is think of someone whose opinion you respect, and ask or imagine, "What would they do in this situation?" You will normally get an immediate answer to the question. It works even down to simple things like picking clothes to wear. Ask someone in your imagination, and the answer will be there.

The beauty of this is that you don't even have to know these people, so long as you have observed their behavior on television, radio or in films. I have successfully used this technique to cut through the dilemmas that frequently come about while on my mission.

# Chapter 7.
# The Loving Power of Soul

### *How to Flow the Loving Power of Soul Into Our Life*

The loving power of Soul is very important, and it is absolutely essential to the success of your mission, but it is also very much misunderstood. Too many people in their weakness strive to have power over others because they have little personal power in their own life. There are many types of power, and in relation to delivering a vision into a mission we can observe some of these powers in the following forms.

From the lowest level is physical power which is the ability to take action when required. It is the energy to move the physical body to a particular place and time. It is the ability to exist in this physical realm.

Then there is emotional power which in its positive sense comes out as enthusiasm. This is absolutely essential in order to succeed in your mission as this energy empowers the physical body and keeps it going.

Next there is causal power which is your ability to stay centered in the "here and now" no matter what the circumstances. Some people find this difficult as their minds are scattered all over the place. Without this essential focus it will be hard to manifest the mission.

Next there is mental power which in its positive sense is the mind's ability to stay focused on the vision, but not so locked in that it ignores the wishes of Soul when a change is necessary.

Finally there is Soul power. **This is the loving power of Soul to BE**. It is the greatest power that exists. It is the power of life itself. You as Soul can, and need, to deliver this loving power into every aspect of your life.

Here is a very simple exercise to strengthen the loving power within you.

### Step 1

*Begin by finding your favorite place for contemplation. Spend a few minutes relaxing, taking your attention off the day, and the problems and worries you may have. Completely free the mind so you can ponder on higher things.*

### Step 2

*Take a few deep breaths, and put your attention on your spiritual heart center which is located in the center of your chest. This is where the pulse of life spreads into your entire being from Soul.*

*From this spiritual heart center imagine that pure white light pours continually vitalizing with loving care your entire being. Take a few minutes to imagine this white light pouring from you as Soul into your entire being vitalizing and refreshing it. Try to imagine the white light which has such strength and power, as being like a mighty ocean pouring such love into your whole being.*

### Step 3

*Now I want you to imagine this loving power expanding beyond your physical body. With each breath you take see it expand into the room you are in. Touching everything in the room with love, it flows out from you in concentric circles similar to the circles created on a pond when you throw a pebble into the water. Imagine the ripples of beautiful white light. Like the crest of a wave flowing outward with each outward breath and returning on the inward breath. You are a source of this divine love, and the love radiates in all directions from you.*

*Now using this same method, imagine the divine love reaching out into the area you live in. Spend a few minutes seeing this life giving force covering the entire neighborhood with loving beauty. Become absorbed with the loving light of Soul as it pulses from your heart center. As you continue to breathe with this loving light see it expand again as it crosses the county lines, and spreads into the whole country, and finally into the whole world. Feel the infinity and vastness of this love that unconditionally emanates from your being. As it lovingly and beautifully touches all things, see them respond with love too.*

*Remain in this heightened state of awareness for a few minutes absorbing and radiating this loving light of Soul. When you are ready, gently return, and open your eyes.*

What this exercise does is work with the loving power of Soul. It helps you to become more of a channel of this energy.

When you become really comfortable with this exercise, try taking it to the next level. To do this we need to use the special, spiritual word HU. So for the next three weeks repeat the exercise as above, but this time on each outward breath sing the beautiful sound of HU in a long drawn out fashion.

As you sing HU, gently place your attention on your inner screen where daydreams occur, and imagine this loving light of Soul flowing from your heart center into the room, the neighborhood and so on, as in the previous exercise. Remember you are not trying to direct the HU to change anything, just simply become the love as you sing HU.

## Honor

Arguments are pointless, simply because if we overcome another with the power of our will, someone else will overcome us sooner or later. The energy that we give out always comes back.

Argumentative people are always in arguments, and since truth is infinite, why argue? What is truth today may not be truth tomorrow. On the other hand a discussion where we can respect the views of others serves us and the other person well. There was a time in the world when honor and respect were important. All too often now the only place we come across these words is in the dictionary. Fewer and fewer people practice them. Yet at the heart of these words is immense personal power so let us take a look at what they actually mean.

If someone was honorable and did things with honor it meant that person had a very high set of ethics. Their values were of the highest order. They did what they said they were going to do, and you knew where you stood with them. It was something that was usually earned because of their behavior. Phrases like, "You can rely on them as they are very honorable," meant a lot in bygone times.

When we operate from a Soul-like state of consciousness, honor is a natural way of living, and people will come to recognize it in you.

The reason why honor is a quality of Soul is because once above the mental level we reach the Soul level. From here on upwards time simply does not exist. This means that whatever Soul imagines happens immediately. There is no kind of double standards where as Soul you say one thing and do another, it simply does not exist. Too often today, some people are looking at what they can get away with, and if they can get one over on you. However, all this does is take power away.

When people operate from a dishonorable state of consciousness they attract dishonorable people as friends, and the downward spiral begins. Taken to the extreme they can ultimately end up in prison with no power, no freedom and no honor.

When we honor the words we utter we begin to move into the realm of personal power. It requires great discipline to only say what we mean, and mean exactly what we say. It takes us out of the realm of saying one thing and doing another, which is all too common nowadays. To be successful in your mission you need to be honorable.

I have listed the seven traits of an honorable person. The spiritual exercise here is to try out these golden traits for the next three months, and chart your progress in your Mission Journal. It is one thing to read it and think it is easy, and a completely different matter to put it into practice.

## The Seven Traits of an Honorable Person

1. *Give freedom to others to determine their own lives.*
2. *Always be kind and never think negative thoughts about others.*
3. *Always do what you say you are going to do.*
4. *Always mean exactly what you say.*
5. *Never go back on your word, unless you tell the other person as soon as you know you cannot fulfill your obligation.*
6. *Only do things you can do with love.*
7. *Never infringe on other people or their property.*

Follow these seven traits, and you will greatly empower your life. It doesn't take much to flow with the loving power of Soul. Like attracts like, and these seven traits of an honorable person are things that give to life. They serve fellow human beings, allowing them to be free and powerful.

I have also found that it is very important to practice these principles in one's own life. That means that you only think about things you are going to do, and not play with fanciful thoughts that just waste energy. Your mission in life, which is about bringing out the true greatness within you, needs every ounce of spiritual energy. Thoughts about things you are never going to do waste energy that could have been empowering you.

## Fantasies Don't Always Serve You

When I was a teenager I used to fantasize about driving a Ferrari. This was my dream car, and I would lose myself in this fantasy for hours. Eventually I lost the car I had to rust and mechanical failure. This was because I was not flowing the loving power of Soul into it. I had no attention on my existing car at all. I would just jump in, drive to work, jump out and pay it no attention. I had no love for it. All my loving attention went into my Ferrari fantasy.

It is great to have the dream, but the dream becomes a fantasy when we don't take the necessary actions to materialize the dream. After a while the fantasy takes on even more spectacular proportions as it drifts further, and further away from reality. Every moment we empower this fantasy, we disempower our lives until the fantasy is everything, and we have nothing. This principle works on everything, even people who fantasize that their partner is someone else. Each time they do this, it disempowers their relationship.

There is a very simple exercise you can do to remove fantasies from your life, enabling you to focus on your true mission and goals in life.

Here is the exercise. List out all the things you want to do in life in the dream column as in the following example...

| # | DREAMS | Short Term Goal | Medium Term Goal | Long Term Goal | Fantasy |
|---|--------|------------|-------------|-----------|---------|
| 1 | Buy a Ferrari | | | YES | |
| 2 | Live in a big dream home | | YES | | |
| 3 | Holiday in Japan | | YES | | |
| 4 | Climb Mount Everest | | | | YES |
| 5 | Swim with dolphins | YES | | | |
| 6 | Dinner with a movie star | | | | YES |

Now go through each dream you have, and decide if it is a goal or a fantasy. Then decide if you want to turn the fantasies into an actual goal or to lovingly remove them from your life.

## Honoring Each Thought and Action

As soon as we take fantasy out of our life we can begin to honor each and every thought we have. By honoring each thought, we can then honor our words. Our words then become an immense source of power because we only say what we mean, and never indulge in idle chit chat and gossip about others. People who spend all day yapping about others tend to have little power in their lives as the constant stream of chat lowers their power. I recall a story from school...

*There was another boy who was always pestering me about one thing or another. He would always try to embarrass me in class, and always hung around me. I was about nine years old, and everyone at school was swearing, using abusive words against each other. Having been brought up as a Christian, I had never uttered a swear word in my life; I felt no need.*

*Anyway, one day when this boy was really pestering me he had taken my school bag, and hidden it somewhere as children will do. I asked him where it was as I had to go home. He refused to tell me and ran away. As he was running down the corridor I seemed to summon some incredible power from somewhere inside me, and I shouted out in this booming voice down the corridor "Tell me where my F.....G bag is now you B.......D!" Now this outburst surprised me, but it scared the living daylights out of this boy. He fell to the ground as if he had been dropped by a gun. He got up off the floor, and came walking back to me, his legs wobbling like Bambi, and said sorry, retrieved my bag, and left. I never had any more trouble from him from that day onwards.*

What this story illustrates is how words carry immense power. For every other kid using swear words there was no power, but at that moment in time a swear word from me expressed my anger and outrage which it would not have done if I had been using swear words all the time.

However, I am not advocating the use of swear words as a source of power as they are very distructive for the user and the recipient.

## Reflect on the Highest

Another way to allow the loving power of Soul to flow into our lives is to ponder on higher things. This might sound like cloud nine stuff, but ten seconds spent reflecting on the qualities of Soul, or something simple that opens your heart to love is better then ten hours worrying about the troubles of the world. Further, the ten seconds in this high state of consciousness will serve the world better than the ten hours of worry.

Eventually you will find your thoughts and words begin to carry this mighty loving power of Soul within them. Your words will become your law. **You will become a law unto yourself, but this carries great responsibility, the responsibility of an honorable person**.

## A Level Playing Field?

When the forefathers established America, some were escaping high taxes and the rule of Monarchy which existed in England. For over one hundred years after the American Constitution had been written it was a land of the free and the brave. What goverment there was, was tiny and did not rule people's lives. However all that began to change when the social fixers began to try to correct and even out the playing field.

Firstly they began to tax people who had worked hard for their living so that they could give to the poor. Sounds noble, but this is an idea that begins from the limited viewpoint that we are not all Soul. It states that we are in fact just our physical bodies and surrounding environment.

How simplistic this viewpoint is. **As Soul we are all equal. That also means <u>we all</u> have the talent to be rich, prosperous, loving, interesting, creative, abundant, infinite, and much more.** But the moment we begin to socially fix people's lives by taking from one group of hard workers to give to another who have not, we infringe upon the rights of Soul. That individual may now not reach their true potential in this lifetime, simply because someone has created an environment that discourages them from having to be the best that they can be. So that person becomes a little more powerless, a little more dependant.

One of the fundamental reasons that we as Soul are in these lower, very coarse worlds is to experience the difficult challenges of life. Each of us as Soul knew what we were doing when we chose this lifetime in this physical world. **It is from the furnace of these challenges that we are honed to become pure in heart, strong in character, and in tune with Soul.** Take away these challenges and we become weak and limp.

I admire people like Martin Luther King. He came here with a mission to inspire people that they are in fact in charge of their lives. That they can make changes as they have the power to be better. He inspired people to believe in their own destiny as bright, positive and powerful.

If we are to become effective individuals we have to decide to begin to flow the loving power of Soul into every aspect of our lives. Here is a simple exercise you can try to take back control over your life. I suggest you write this down in your Mission Journal.

All you need to do is list all the people, all the places, all the animals, and all the objects you have abdicated (surrendered) power to. A key to knowing what these are is to write down all the things you think you **HAVE TO DO.** Write as many things that come to mind.

Here is a totally random sample:

1. *I HAVE to wake up to feed my cat at 4am.*
2. *I HAVE to pay my taxes.*
3. *I HAVE to wash my car.*
4. *I HAVE to let my partner do the shopping.*
5. *I HAVE to listen while my boss shouts at me.*
6. *I HAVE to take personal abuse.*
7. *I HAVE to let my partner make the big decisions.*
8. *I HAVE to be home by 6pm.*
9. *I HAVE to eat all my food my partner cooks, or else.*
10. *I HAVE to be nice to Bob for an easy life.*
11. *I HAVE to stay in this loveless marriage, and hope.*
12. *I HAVE to let Bob pick the television channels.*

Now, when you have completed your list go through each item on the list and ask yourself, "Did I lovingly and freely abdicate my power or was it taken away from me?" To make things simple, put a "√" beside each item where you lovingly abdicated power.

Then go back through the list, and this time decide whether you are going to take back the power. In this case use a "T" to signify taking back control. So you now have a list of actions.

When you decide to take back control, do it gently step by step. Write it down in your Mission Journal and take wise actions. That means asking yourself, "What is the best way to take back control?" There is no hurry so take time to reflect upon this. You will find that Soul will work with you and Divine Spirit to help you take back control.

Usually it is much easier than it appears at first. Remember this concept about Fear as **F**alse **E**vidence **A**ppearing **R**eal. What you will discover time and time again is that the loving power of Soul will overcome all obstacles, and level any playing field. However you are the one who must take the action, and you will know what the action is by the moment you take it. Also, never lock yourself into a particular action. As you take action, you as Soul are learning the best way, so if you get a nudge to stop or change direction, that's okay too.

Taking action builds great spiritual strength and wisdom. Eventually you become a spiritual eagle, free, strong, and in love with all life. Everytime you take back some power, and gain more control over your life, your mission will evolve with more clarity and strength.

## The Power of Action

If we constantly expect others to do things for us, when we can do them ourselves, we will tend to move through life in weakness. **However, when we hold the attitude that we are the one who takes action, who moves, who changes to get to the goal, it allows us to move through life in power and agility.**

## Success Consciousness

There are many people who have a dream. They know what their purpose in life is, but they just don't seem to be able to get there. Everything seems to conspire to make them fail at every step. The harder they try the more difficult it becomes. This is due to the failure consciousness. It can be caused by taking each knock and fall in life too seriously. In doing so it has created an expectation of failure in the subconscious to the point that their best efforts just unwind before their very eyes. They know that they are close to manifesting their dream but how? They are like the potential high jumper, who stands underneath the high jump bar, and wonders how to clear the bar. Inside there is a deep knowingness that they can jump this bar, but how? Only by watching the experts take a running leap do they realize how it can be done.

Just a simple change of attitude is all that is required. If the attitude stays the same, the same old failure patterns will continue. There isn't one set way to achieve a goal. Success comes from an attitude that is, "As light as laughter, yet strong as steel". This means never allowing emotions to get out of control, and never allowing the mind to lock you into a one way course of action.

**Sooner or later you will notice that you begin to develop a very special and personal philosophy. This philosophy comes from the heart of Soul, and it is your own.** It is not like a man-made philosophy that you need to think about. You are it; your every action flows with it.

## Superstition

Do you hold any superstitions? They can be one of the most controlling and debilitating thought forms we hold. The positive superstitions tend to be life enforcing, but they still create a degree of control over our life that is unnecessary.

In theatres all around the world, the actors and actresses have to be told to "break a leg" before they go on as this brings them good luck, but what if there was no one to say these words to them. They would then begin to expect disaster, and what happens? A disaster befalls them, like they trip over or forget their lines. It is best to live with no superstitions at all. There are enough things in this world trying to control the individual without creating more.

In some countries around the world, Friday the 13th is very unlucky so thousands of people just stay in bed, even if it means losing a day's pay. I recall an incident in England...

*I looked out of the office window to see the window cleaner put a ladder in the street, and angle it up to the second story of the building to clean the windows. It meant that the ladder straddled the pavement where people were walking. Now in England walking under a ladder means very bad luck to the superstitious. So on this particular day there was a very old lady in her eighties I guess. She had a walking frame to help her stay upright, and she moved very slowly.*

*Well as you can guess, she came up to this ladder, and obviously, being superstitious she had to make a decision, either walk under the ladder which was easy or take her life in her own hands, and gamble with the busy traffic on the road. So she chose to gamble with the busy traffic. I watched almost in horror as this lady who could hardly walk, chanced her life, and almost got knocked down several times by speeding traffic, because she could not just walk around the base of the ladder, but had to go around two cars that fenced in the ladder.*

One way out of superstitions is to slowly make a conscious effort to declare to yourself that your energy is greater than the superstition, that you have gone beyond the limitations of yesterday. Then you have to believe it and acknowledge it. After all, which is greater, a myth or the <u>LOVING POWER OF YOU AS SOUL?</u>

## Effective Human Beings

When we deliver this loving power of Soul into our lives, it begins to transform us into effective human beings. **This loving power is the momentum we need to propel our vision into a mission**. It makes the difference between living in a fantasy, and living out our mission, our special purpose here in life.

**This loving power of Soul is our mighty and unlimited energy to CREATE!** As Soul we all share the highest qualities of the divine source, which are love, freedom, wisdom, and power. All of these qualities flow within us as mighty oceans, and as Soul we can flow these qualities into any aspect of our lives.

This loving power of Soul is also a neutral force. The keys to unlock and flow it into our life are love, wisdom, and creativity. Every single thought and action we take draws in some way on this loving power. When used wisely it can make every single dream we have a reality, and most of all, it will turn Soul's vision into a mission. It can take us from this moment in time to the high states of Soul Realization, and into the heart of God Realization.

You can see the people who are truly working with this loving power of Soul. Their lives are vibrant and filled with rich experiences. They also tend to be those who live their dreams.

In conclusion I would like to mention this. Whenever we join love and power together to take action that is inspired with love, we are working with the greatest power in the whole universe.

Consider this: You are at home, the floor needs to be swept. You hate sweeping the floor, but you realize that your spouse is coming home later and you want a tidy house for them. What happens is that the love flows into your heart, and you suddenly have the energy and enthusiam to sweep the floor. That's all it takes. **Start with love and you'll have the power to manifest your mission.**

# Chapter 8.
# Cycles of Energy
## How to Understand the Flow of Energy
## That Creates Experiences in Our Life

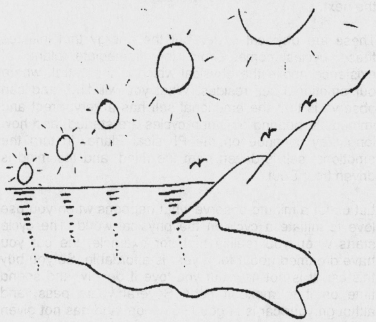

As we begin to embark upon our mission it is worth just pondering for a while on cycles (rhythms or flows of energy), as well as how they affect our direction and possible decisions we are likely to make.

For everything there is a cycle, and every cycle is a season in which it is positive then negative. You can see this in everything from the weather where you have a high pressure zone that eventually gets replaced by a low pressure zone. You can see it in people around you. Even the mid-life crisis is a cycle that Soul creates to make us change, and commence new cycles of experience. It comes out in small ways like when people are happy one day, sad the next. Tired one minute, vitalized the next. Even things we buy have cycles, like cars that are shining and new one year, and rust buckets the next.

These are physical cycles but the energy that initiates these cycles comes from the immediate plane of existence above the physical which is the astral, where our emotional self resides. What you will find, and can observe is that the emotional self has a very direct and immediate bearing on when cycles are started, and how long they continue on the Physical Plane. In turn the emotional self is driven from the mind, and the mind is driven from Soul.

Let us for a minute observe what happens when you use love to initiate a cycle in the physical world. The cycle starts when you realize that, for example, the car you have dreamed about for a year is affordable. So you buy this car. It is not new but you love it deeply, and spend time on it to make it right. Several years pass, and although your car is in good condition, and has not given you any trouble you need a new one for various reasons. The moment you decide to buy a new car, and your loving attention passes from your existing car to this shining new number in the show room a new cycle begins.

This new cycle is the negative cycle for the existing car, and a positive cycle for the new car. You have effectively withdrawn the love for the existing car, and assigned it to the new car. If the existing car is old it is likely to begin to break down. Faults start to show, problems arise, and what was a simple sale of the existing car becomes an expensive garage job to put it right. Of course this is not true in every case. It depends to the degree in which the object in question can withstand the withdrawal of the love you were giving it because feeling directly affects matter.

People who are very negative about life or dislike various people tend to initiate a number of negative cycles in their lives, and every cycle must complete. People who are positive about life and love life tend to initiate positive cycles. Then each positive cycle initiates another so when one cycle turns negative their attention is on the next positive cycle so they tend to experience far less negativity in their lives.

This is why putting your attention on your mission at least three times a day is beneficial as it initiates three positive wave fronts of love everyday, and each wave will deliver you closer to realizing your true destiny. The main driving force above the emotions is the mind. This is the realm of thought. So if you are to quicken and make certain that you will manifest this mission or any goals you have in life you will need to flow as many loving thoughts of success through your consciousness as possible. This creates a habit for you of success. Also look for things that inspire and encourage you in your mission as this too initiates new positive cycles.

Finally above the mind is Soul on the Soul Plane. From this high state of consciousness Soul can see all and knows the best route to take. This is why it is so important to "ask the right question" as mentioned earlier. This invites Soul to take a greater part in your life.

Soul selects the right thoughts that initiate the right cycles to put you in the right place at the right time to manifest your mission via the best route. We can experience Soul guiding us this way when from a random bunch of thoughts on nothing in particular we suddenly latch onto a thought that for some reason inspires us. This is Soul highlighting a thought, and the moment your attention falls on this thought a new cycle is initiated.

**Always, check that it is not your emotions that have initiated this thought by seeing how light and breezy it all feels.** If the thought feels heavy then it is from the emotions and is probably not that inspired.

Before I take any action I say to myself, "Okay I am Soul. Are these actions the action of Soul? Will it make a difference for the better? Is this the best I can do?"

After about a month of constantly doing this it becomes a natural part of your subconscious so you will not even have to think it. It will be a natural part of how you act. Eventually you create a CAN DO consciousness based on the highest ethics, and the success cycle becomes a natural part of you.

## Overcoming Resistance

This CAN DO consciousness is very important. You will need it to overcome the inertia (resistance to change) as your life changes to embrace your mission. The degree to which you will experience inertia depends on how long you have been in your current situation, how much loving power you can flow into your life, and how well you can hold the vision of the mission. You only experience inertia when you make a change in your direction. So stand still and you never notice it. Make a change and everything lines up against you. It is just like the seat belt in the car. You can move forward and backward slowly, but any sudden changes in direction, and the belt jerks you to a halt.

Here are six tips to overcome inertia...

1. *A very important factor in overcoming inertia is persistence. That means never ever give up on your vision. This allows Soul to work with Divine Spirit to better orchestrate your future.*

2. *Make the changes you need to make at your pace, not someone else's. Racing ahead to keep up with someone else or to match someone else's success can create inertia.*

3. *Always do everything with love. Soul is so filled with love and beauty it takes just a moment to flow this love and beauty into your life, and into your actions.*

4. *Work on your comfort zones if you feel that some are holding you back. Review Chapter Two again.*

5. *Look for ways to simplify your life. Complex lives experience the most inertia when change is necessary. So look at all the aspects of your life that you feel are complicated, and spend time on removing complexities. In particular look at simplifying or removing events and situations that are unnecessarily interlocked.*

6. *When something goes wrong, ignore the negative stuff and focus on the positive. Look for the loving gift in every difficulty. It is in the adverse situations that your inner strengths come forth and really shine.*

I recall a story that illustrates how this inertia works, and how we can all overcome it by persistence, and looking for the positive...

*I was working as a computer consultant, and I had just won a contract to teach a senior management team how to make effective use of computers in their business. The course was to be very comprehensive, and cover a number of topics specific to their industry. The evening before, I was completing the course booklets and working on the computer to polish the final drafts. All the handouts and overhead transparencies were in this one file on the computer, about eighty pages of documentation. A friend of mine suggested that I spell check the document before I printed the first draft.*

*So I clicked on the spell check icon on the computer screen, and the printer burped into action, printed the first line then stopped. I waited and nothing happened. It slowly dawned on me that the computer had frozen up. I had no backup of my work. I had no print out of my work. I was staring at a week's work flushed down the toilet. It was a disaster, but in a flash Soul was working to resolve the situation.*

*I managed to laugh at the situation for several minutes, which really helped to lighten up the atmosphere, and I was able to feel that I could recreate the eighty page document if I started immediately. I worked through the night, and by 3am I had completed the document. It was shorter; just sixty pages long. I had several printouts, and several backups of the document. The shortage of pages made me feel like the teenager who does his first service on his motorbike only to find upon re-assembly that there are several screws left in his hand that were not there when he started.*

*However, the document was sufficient, and the presentation the next day went better than ever. The loving gift in the situation was that I knew the document inside out, and did not need any props. Also, I was able to emphasize to the group the need for document security and backups. This, unbeknown to me, was a particular concern for this company.*

*Had I flown into a rage I would have never completed the document or learned the lessons hidden in the adversity.*

## Sensing Cycles in Life

As you unfold spiritually along your path, it is likely you will begin to see cycles in life beyond the knowledge of most people. This allows you to take wise actions, and choose which cycles in life you initiate and experience, or even which cycles you need to balance and conclude in past or current situations. Your mission in life is a major cycle, but there are many more minor cycles in the goals you set, and qualities or talents you choose to flow into your life. It is important that you choose cycles that support the direction you want your life to flow in.

## Expectation

Expectation is a very powerful energy, and negative expectations can devastate our life. How many times have we heard people say, "I fear the worst." followed by, "My worst fears have come true." or "The thing I feared most has come upon me." These negative expectations tend to come true because they are so powerful.

Positive expectations on the other hand can bring fantastic results since they open you up to unlimited opportunities that Soul is orchestrating. Putting your attention on Soul's vision manifests the mission, and a whole host of other positive cycles as the vision is infused with all the loving qualities of Soul.

## Preparing the Ground

If by now you know what your mission in life is, then you should also have a set of goals to really bring this into an outer expression. Then it is time to start the physical cycle. This is like olympic relay running where the person who is to receive the baton to continue the race starts running before the other person with the baton gets to him. This means that the receiver of the baton never has to start from scratch, and receives the baton while running. Then just powers home to cross the finish line.

We can do the same here in the physical world simply by acting as if the goal we seek is already here. Or we begin to act "as if" we are working with particular talents, values, or qualities of Soul. Acting "as if" begins the physical cycle so that when all the inner preparation is ready it will gently blend into what we have already started on the outer. However, great responsibility is required.

If for instance your mission is to become a wealthy merchant ship owner shipping spices from India to New York, it does not mean you start spending money as if you are wealthy. It means taking time to see what merchant ship owners do. Perhaps you could order the same monthly magazine merchant ship owners read. Then you could order the spice growers monthly magazine or associate with merchant shippers. Drink coffee in the same coffee shops where you know they go. Become interested with the detail of what they do, and as you do this **imagine yourself as if you are already there**. You could go down to the docks, look at a ship coming in, and imagine that this is your first spice shipment. **Feel the exhilaration and sense of completeness**.

This is just an example, but it gets the point across that acting "as if" you are already there starts a cycle to get you there quicker.

## Honoring Mistakes and Failure

There is a cycle of energy that flows between positive and negative events. The Chinese represented this with the Ying and Yang. This cycle, this changing balance is caused by the life force, or if you like, the divine love of God, splitting into two currents.

It splits the moment it enters into the lower worlds; the worlds of the mind, emotion and physical matter. The split is subtle at first, but becomes more dramatic the lower we get, until we arrive at this Physical Plane. Here this dual current, which flows through you, me and all of life in order to sustain us, allows us to express the greatest creativity.

However we can never create something that is perfect. Too many times we forget that some of the greatest advances in human civilization were achieved by someone making a mistake. There is no dishonor in making mistakes, in fact it is more of a loving gift from Soul. If we never fail, we will never succeed. In each mistake there is an opportunity for success. So instead of beating up on ourselves when we achieve less than we set out to, we need to embrace the failure with love and curiosity, simply because everything in life comes to us as a gift.

It is the same as in the example I gave earlier in the book about the two people in a garden. One sees a garden full of weeds, rocks and insects, the other sees a perfumed delight filled with blue dragonflies, ladybirds and beautiful flowers. Yet it is the same garden. One person, as it were, sees it as a "mistake", the other embraces it with love and curiosity, and it is they that experience this beautiful breath of divine love.

Everyone in life, whether knowingly or not is trying to balance the duality of divine love. Some become easygoing. Some of us become difficult and a million other combinations. We are like captains of ships, sailing on this sea of divine love. Some have become masters of their ships. Others are tilting at ninety degrees, without ever realizing it. Others are completely out of control. Ultimately we begin to understand the sea and wind, then begin to move towards the balanced state. This is being non-judgemental, being neither for nor against anything in life, but always seeking the highest in everything. Look for the love in every activity, and live life with a curious loving heart. Then every failure and mistake emerges as a loving opportunity for progress. If we hold this attitude to life, then a serene beauty and love will begin to flow in the heart.

# Chapter 9.
# Soul's Guiding Light

## How to Allow Your Life to Breathe With the Loving Guidance of Soul.

To really succeed with your mission you will need to be in tune with the guidance that flows from Soul. This does not mean that life will be like a bed of roses, but it means that whatever experience we go through we are more likely to recognize the learning, and therefore experience greater freedom. It is also much more likely that by flowing the guidance of Soul out into life, we will be in the exact place at the exact time to reap the best benefit from whatever situation we may find ourselves in.

Soul resides on the Soul Plane and is totally immersed in the celestial light. This light is pure divine love, and the light vibrates with a beautiful sound, the voice of God. Soul resonating in this sound and light is perfectly in tune with Divine Spirit which is the all pervasive (everywhere) essence of God that is in all life, and supports all life in its every existence, in every dimension, in its every expression.

**Soul is in perfect harmony with this divine essence. It works at all times for our highest good**. It is just that so often we don't realize it. When we set out to find our mission, Soul began to work in an infinite number of ways for our highest good.

This is a very important point for it means that we are always getting guidance from Soul all of the time, and Soul is getting guidance from the divine source. It is also true that the more we strive with our mission by gaining valuable experiences, the more expansive and courageous Soul becomes. So our consciousness begins to shift upward, and at times it will seem as if we have touched the heart of the divine source because of the way things are working out in our life. It sometimes feels like a waterfall of blessings pouring into every situation.

The divine source does not differentiate who will receive guidance or blessings in life. The nasty thug on the street corner receives as much guidance as you. The only difference is that the thug is not tuned into it, so misses it, which is why he is still a thug on the street corner.

To receive guidance in our life we need three qualities which are love, gratitude and humility. You are probably very familiar with love and gratitude, but our Western culture has a lot of difficulty with humility because of the ego. However, a simple way to practice humility is not to put yourself down, but to acknowledge that everyone is Soul and all Souls are equal. I recall a story from my past about humility...

*I had just landed myself a prestigious job in a bank. On the Monday morning I put on my new suit with my new shirt and tie, and splashed on my expensive cologne. I arrived at work, and had to go up to the fifth floor, so I got in the elevator. I was the only one in it. The elevator stopped on the second floor, and three workmen got in. As they left the elevator one of the guys farted (please excuse the English) and it was very smelly. The elevator doors shut, and I found it hard to breathe as the odor clashed with my cologne, and it was just an awful smell. I thought to myself thank God I am early, and no one else is here as yet. Then to my horror the elevator stopped on the fourth floor. My heart pounded! People would think that it was me who created this smell. Well my horror was well founded as the doors opened, and in walked my new boss. I was so ashamed and embarrassed about this smell. It was just horrible and he immediately noticed, and just managed to say morning before turning away into the corner of the elevator for fresh air.*

Well this taught me something about humility. There I was all pompous, and feeling better than everyone else, in my new suit and expensive cologne. In that state Soul was unable to work with me, so it orchestrated a situation to pop my ego which was the size of a planet, and it worked. I was very grateful later (much later)!

## Planning

It is important to develop a short, medium, and long term plan for your life. The short term plan should be the most detailed. A little less detail is required for the medium term plan, and just a skeleton framework is required for the long term plan.

Holding a vision and expecting it to manifest into a mission just won't work. It needs careful planning, action and effort. Allow your plans to breathe with love. Never plan every detail of every minute, of everyday, else you will choke the plan to death. When you have a short, medium, and long term plan it allows Divine Spirit to work more closely with your life so that transitions are smoother. You will find your life rolling on like gentle hills that grace the landscape, rather than jagged rocks, which is how it can be when you don't plan.

## True Surrender

Life for some people can be filled with stress and worry, but all this does is lower the consciousness to the emotional level. Soul never experiences stress or worry, and it is very important that you try to avoid these lower states of consciousness. The moment you descend into these negative pits you cut yourself off from the inspiration and guidance of Soul. No matter how precarious your journey in life may seem, never give up your faith in yourself as Soul, for it is Soul that will bring you through the darkest night of your life.

The easiest way to get rid of stress and worry is by surrendering it to the care of Divine Spirit.

All you have to do is this...

1. *Write it down if you can in your Mission Journal.*
2. *Do as much as possible to solve the problem FIRST!!!*
3. *Surrender it to Divine Spirit by saying something like "I am Soul, therefore I surrender this problem into the care of Divine Spirit. I know it will work out". (Say this with love and knowingness in your heart).*
4. *Get on with your life, and don't think about the problem.*

Once you have done as much as you can do to solve the problem, and then surrendered it to Divine Spirit, Soul will begin to work with Spirit to untangle the complexities and find the best way forward. You may get your answer by a knowingness to take a particular action, or through a dream, or from some event that will be obvious to you that you can proceed. However make sure you have first of all done as much as you can.

One thing that should be of inspiration is that Divine Spirit is working for your own highest good in every situation past, present and future. So when you are home at the weekends pondering upon the problems facing you at work, Spirit is working to help you through the problems you face. So as you reflect, rather than worry, upon a difficult problem, you suddenly receive divine inspiration. **Divine Spirit never stops working for Soul's highest good.**

## Blessings in Life

The blessings of Spirit are available for all Souls, and flow freely, but we don't all experience them. In comparison to a rock, you as a human being have a greater capacity to realize or perceive the blessings of

Spirit. But how many of us choose to remain like the rocks. To receive the blessings of Spirit we need to loosen up and live life to the fullest. This way we experience life. It is in each experience that the blessings of life are hidden.

## Direction

Guidance comes in the way you least expect it. You may expect things to work out one way, and they work out in exactly the opposite way. Divine Spirit always works with this infinite view on life.

In Chapter Five which dealt with turning the vision into a mission I discussed this simple method of holding the vision. That is to say you place your attention on the goal or quality of Soul you are seeking to manifest. This method works as long as you hold the vision because as long as you do this Soul begins to work with Divine Spirit to figure out, and orchestrate the interconnecting steps that take you from where you are now to your destiny.

The route is never a straight line because Soul will work out the best route that takes in the most **relevant learning you need to manifest the mission**. It is much like an aircraft "en route from Paris to Ohio." The plane will fly a route that goes north to Iceland, climb in altitude to 55,000 feet to save fuel, and then fly south down the coast of Canada into America and then southwest to Ohio. The route is not a straight line, but the pilot knows the most efficient route that makes use of winds, high pressure zones, etc. so that the plane can land at the designated time.

In a nut shell, all you have to do is...

1. *Hold the vision.*
2. *Always be prepared to take action.*
3. *Be courageous.*
4. *Live your daily life with great expectation.*
5. *Trust in Divine Spirit to work things out for your highest good.*

## Night Time Dreams

I would also like to talk a little about dreams. We all have dreams whether we are conscious of them occurring or not. A dream is just activity, much like physical activity, that occurs on either the Astral, Casual, Mental, Etheric or Soul Planes.

Once you start working towards your mission it is likely that your dream life will become amplified. People who don't remember dreams still get guidance, but mostly through nudges and waking dreams. These are the daytime occurrences where something or some event or some image suddenly takes on spiritual meaning, much like in a dream. Another point is that when you are smoothly moving in the direction you are aiming you don't necessarily receive dream guidance.

When you write down your dreams (waking or night time) leave a space to note down one or more of these points:

1. How you felt the moment you awoke.
2. How you felt about the dream during the day.
3. How the dream felt at the end of the day.
4. What experiences you are going through in life.
5. What you think this dream means.
6. What you think actually happened.

The dream worlds or inner planes can be very friendly places, with many people able and willing to assist you in your quest, and guide you in your mission. Dreams are a great source of guidance.

A common dream to have when you radically change your life or attitude is that of seeing your own death, and burial. This is death of your old self and old ways so the new you can emerge. However, it is important to learn your own dream symbols. Practice writing down the six points on the preceding page, as this will help you understand the dream language. After a few months of consistent effort you will begin to know what your dreams mean. **Your dream language is unique to you**.

I would also encourage you to write down dreams as this completes the cycle and balances the energy from the dream, which can be unsettling in some instances.

We tend to dream in symbols when we are unable to accept the direct truth. It is a feature of our inner bodies to symbolize dreams, and it is all under the control of Soul. However, the more courageous we become the less symbols we see, and we begin to perceive direct truth. **Ultimately we move from trying to see what is truth to being the knower of truth.**

# Chapter 10.
# The Ecstasy of Soul

## Experience the Deep Joy of Soul
## in Everyday Life

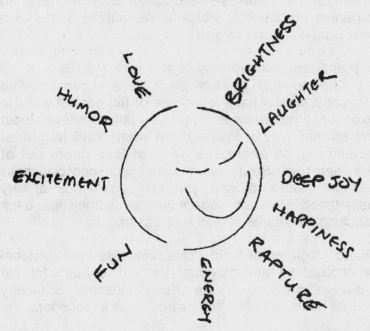

Soul is naturally a happy being. It always has been, and always will be happy. In fact, the joy that Soul experiences is beyond human description, and has to be experienced to know what it is. Many people have glimpses of varying degrees of Soul's joyful nature. For instance when you spontaneously laugh about something or a situation, rather than at someone, the laughter ripples through from Soul to the point that sometimes you are unable to stop laughing.

When we are in touch with Soul, and find ourselves in a serious situation we can tend to burst out in laughter. Children especially do this. Consider the dinner table when you are in situations where you are meant to behave, and be serious, and a lot is riding on your behavior. It does not take much to burst into uncontrollable laughter, especially if you have to suppress the laughter which is like putting Soul into a box. Something has to give.

Joy and laughter are very high qualities of Soul. If we learn how to laugh at situations in life, and generally find life funny, we will have found one of the easiest ways to experience ourselves as Soul. Very little is known about the spiritual side of laughter, but **when Soul laughs at something, an enormous wave of love pours out of the heart of Soul.** From here your consciousness becomes elevated, and you can experience a very heightened state of consciousness, sometimes even touching the shores of God Realization.

These high states of consciousness are seldom recognized by the individual for long enough for the individual to hold that state of consciousness. But every little bit helps. I recall a story when I was a teenager...

*It was the summer holidays and time to build our special go-carts. It was a customary ritual to build the biggest and fastest go-cart in town. This particular year my go-cart was big, almost the size of a small car. It had the customary four wheels, but this time I had put a large wooden box on the framework to act as a cabin facing forward.*

*On one fateful summer day I took this cart, which was very heavy, to the top of a hill on a main road to race down the hill with a friend. We both set off down this hill probably reaching speeds of 25 miles per hour which to a kid of my size was very fast. As I overtook my friend down this hill one of the ropes controlling the steering broke. This made my cart swerve violently to the right, leave the sidewalk and veer out onto the main road. Somehow I missed several cars by inches and smashed into the sidewalk on the other side of the road. The impact catapulted the cart, and me inside this box, into the brick wall. It was a scene of devastation, and I lay on the ground covered in wood, wheels and extreme pain.*

*I was unable to move, but my friend ran across the road to me, and just began to laugh. In fact he was laughing so much he was unable to help me. He was completely beside himself with laughter. At first I was angry, but after a while I began to smile, then laugh, and the more I laughed the less pain I felt, and the happier I was. I climbed out of the mess and looked down at it laughing as much as my friend.*

Laughter from Soul always changes your perspective on the most negative situation. Indeed it has the ability to heal mental and physical illness simply because of the love that pours from the heart of Soul when we genuinely laugh.

To succeed in your mission, I believe that laughter forms a very special ingredient. It allows you to expand your consciousness beyond the daily humdrum of life. As you begin to pull the vision of Soul into your consciousness you will begin to experience these ecstatic states of consciousness.

Indeed the phase you go through called the "Busy Fool" is caused by you experiencing the ecstasy of Soul, and many people find themselves laughing at the slightest thing in life. They are riding on this incredible wave of love and happiness. **If we take our focus off the negative things in life our consciousness naturally drifts into higher states of awareness where there is more happiness, laughter and a deep sense of joy**.

There are a number of things that on a daily basis try and get the attention of the five negative traits of the human consciousness. In doing so our attention is drawn away from the ecstasy of Soul. These negative traits are:

1. *Anger*
2. *Greed*
3. *Lust*
4. *Vanity*
5. *Attachment*

Life is all about balance. We need to make sure we don't overindulge our attention in pursuits that saturate our consciousness with these negative traits. It will certainly slow down our mission and/or cloud the perception of Soul's vision. Dwelling in these states of consciousness takes our attention away from the ecstatic states of Soul.

There are some Eastern spiritual paths that preach to their followers that they must erase these negative traits, but to survive in these lower worlds we need them. The trick is never to be dominated by them, and never be led by them.

A lot of the media is dominated by these negative traits. The news programs lean on the negative side of life and the end result is that more and more people are living in fear of their lives. As long as they hold the consciousness of fear they will attract fearful situations into their lives.

A friend of mine who has stopped watching television said to me that they might as well call many of these investigation programs by new names like "Tonight on: Why There's No Point in Going On" or "Tonight on: You Should Be Worried" or "Tonight on: We Have Discovered That YOU Are Doomed, There Is No More Hope". Although he meant it humorously there is a serious point here, and the media need to take responsibility for the control they are having over people's lives. This world is a learning ground, and we are all learning fast. Fear is a challenge that people have to face and overcome. **Love is the special ingredient that dissolves all fear.**

Fear shuts down the heart center, and so we lose touch with the higher guidance of Soul. Then fate leads our lives rather than the loving guidance of Soul. The next time you listen to a news program ask yourself if it lifts your consciousness or lowers it. The next time you listen to music ask the same question, and ask this question of the people you associate with.

Here are three suggestions to help put the bright sparkle of Soul back into your life...

1. *This is so simple, but often overlooked. Find a song or tune that you really love beause it opens your heart with love. Then as you go through your day, hum or whistle the tune to yourself. It is amazing the difference that this makes. It is like spiritual oil that makes the day run smoothly.*

2. *Try reflecting on the joy and beauty within the heart of Soul. This in turn allows our lives to flow with more joy.*

3. *Find a way to share love with someone everyday. This can be in kind thought, or in action. Doing an act of kindness everyday will allow more of Soul's love, Soul's loving power, and Soul's loving laughter to flow into your life. What we unconditionally give to life comes back to us a thousand fold every time.*

In conclusion I would like to suggest this. The next time you have a problem, don't approach it with fear and worry. Instead try approaching the problem with joy, laughter, love and Soul's natural curiosity. **NO PROBLEM CAN EVER WITHSTAND THE ASSAULT OF JOY, LAUGHTER, LOVE AND SOUL'S CURIOSITY.** These qualities of Soul easily lift you above the problem and allow you to have an infinite viewpoint on the problem. From this elevated viewpoint, so many more solutions are possible.

# Chapter 11.
# The Eternal Essence
## Becoming What You Truly Are

This is about our ability to be truly successful in life. It is not about how rich we can become. Success is about achieving what we originally set out to achieve, then being able to hold onto that achievement, and do more with it as we please, until we decide it is time to change.

This is why success is a journey, and not a destination. Many people have a tiny success in something, and then claim they have been successful. **However unless we have been tested by adversity it is impossible to truly say we are successful.**

It is like flying a fighter plane. Unless we have been in battle we cannot claim any title to being a great fighter pilot. The pilots who survived the Second World War did so because they had the skill and good judgement to evade the enemy. It had nothing to do with luck and everything to do with their alert state of consciousness.

This is the same with our mission. If we can see ourselves as completing each stage of the mission, then we will. If we see problems then we will meet problems. If at the first obstacle we fall and complain, we are in for a rough ride. To succeed takes staying power. The journey has to be more important than any small problem we may encounter.

We become like the mountain climber who may trip and fall, but never gives up. The glory and exhilaration of victory outweighs obstacles that befall the path to the top of the mountain. I think that the traits of a mountain climber are very relevant. They are also the seven qualities of someone living in the essence of their mission:

## 1. Hold a Strong Vision

This is the key to changing the direction of our life, and it is so important to **hold this vision no matter what, when, why or how our personal circumstances may change.** It is also likely that our situation will change, old things will drop away to make room for the new.

## 2. Self Discipline

This is so often overlooked, but self discipline is at the heart of a good life. It is essential if old traits are to be broken.

## 3. Staying Power

There is a rare kind of steel within each of us. Don't be scared to show it. Success comes to those who stay the course, and don't give up at the first hurdle. I recall an incident several years ago when I went for a job interview.

*I drove to the interview in my new BMW car. The last visitors parking space was next to the Manager's car, and his car was also a BMW. Unfortunately, I could not get out of the driver's door as the space was too tight, so I straddled across to the passenger side, and squeezed out the passenger door. Just then I heard a gigantic ripping sound. I looked down to see my trousers' inside leg had split from the crotch down to both knees. They were flapping like the leather chaps a cowboy wears. Now this was the second interview for this job. I had it in the bag according to my agent, but looking down at my flapping trousers, I panicked. Out of embarrassment, I squeezed back into the car, and sped off. I lacked staying power, but one learns pretty quickly that we have to hold to the course, and not give in to weakness, but strengthen ourselves with love, and be able to laugh at our mistakes.*

## 4. Build a Good Plan

There is always time to make a good plan of what you are going to do. However planning only works if we work the plan on a daily basis by taking action when we need to. We need to keep going over the plan in our mind until it becomes a mental framework. Also we should never make our plan rigid. We need to allow it to unfold as circumstances change.

## 5. Develop Your Bounce Back Factor

As you move into living your mission, you become like the mountain climber. You stand at the top of the mountain filled with exhilaration, and a true sense of achievement. The sun shines, you relax, there are no clouds, life is in balance. Many successful people find themselves in this position. From here life is easy. Then from nowhere, the wind of change can begin to blow. Soul attracts this wind of change. It needs to continue to grow, to experience at an ever greater depth its true talents and qualities. So life begins to change and Soul grows within each change.

For the unwary, the wind of change can be like an avalanche. It carries them down to the bottom of the mountain. But rather than a disaster, this can be a golden moment. Soul is so alive as this change is taking place. If our belief in the vision and the journey is more important than any upset along the way then we will live to climb an even higher mountain the next day. A strong belief is what it takes to be the "come back kid". To always bounce back no matter what the circumstance. Hold the vision and your belief in the vision. **With this attitude, no matter what challenges you, it will seem as if you have never left the mountain top.**

## 6. Wisdom

This is being smart, using good judgement, and working from your highest state of consciousness possible at all times. Always being prepared to look at something from a new viewpoint.

## 7. Love

This is doing every action with heart. It is the one thing that will make us the best and give the best to life.

To become the essence of Soul's vision means having the expectation that we will succeed, and if this means disassociating with those who pull us down at our every turn, then so be it. There will always be more positive people to fill the gap. **As you begin to align your life to your mission you will begin to experience the awesome power of the entire universe aligning behind you, beside you, and preparing the way ahead of you.**

**It is as if everything and all situations are conspiring to help you to succeed.** You will notice it in the small things in life, and in the grand scheme of things. This occurs when your mission makes a difference for the better in life.

These lower worlds experience constant creation. Nothing is permanent. This is why becoming the essence of your mission is so important. Once you become the essence you become the creator. If circumstances change to the point that you have to get up and move on, then so be it. You move on, and the moment you set down again everything in life is conspiring to bring about your outer mission once more. It is a natural part of you, like attracting like.

Living in the essence also means moving through each day in loving balance and power. A great way to achieve this is by starting each day with a short HU song. It is a simple love song from the heart of Soul to the divine source.

The HU will harmonize you with life, so you will find that even in the darkest moments you will be flowing with life. Flowing with life is not weak and wishy washy, but it is strong. There is no greater force, no greater power than that which sustains all of life, in all the universes of God, seen and unseen. **By tuning in to this force you become it. You never lose your individuality, but you gain your freedom; <u>the freedom to be as you choose</u>**.

There are many who catch a fleeting glimpse of the splendor of Soul's qualities in their lives, and they then set out to have everything in life. Their thirst to have everything and own everything can never be quenched, whether they are aware of it or not. They are constantly hoarding earthly riches as each possession they acquire reminds them of the celestial beauty of Soul. However they have become a slave to the effects.

Better are those who seek first to become the celestial beauty and light of Soul by living in the vision of Soul. For these people, everything in life is theirs. They are the ones who recognize that to hold onto something serves only to lose it.

Possessions, be they animate or inanimate, live only as long as they are free. If someone asks you for something, and you suddenly think of the loss, then it will be a loss, but if you think only of their gain then you will receive equally as much as you gave, and more.

The source of all things is within, and it is important to remind ourselves of this. It is the freedom we afford everything in our life that serves to allow the abundance of Soul to manifest in our life. Non-attachment is at the heart of abundance, and for abundance to flow through our lives we need to ease up, free up, and enter into the infinite flow of life.

When you drive your life from Soul, you become the effect of nothing. Life becomes centered in the moment, and every moment builds upon the last one with love, wisdom and truth. Divine love expresses the creative force in your life, and only by loving what you do can you experience a greater measure of life. In the same way that looking for the best in people brings out the best in them and in you, this too is true for everything we do in life. Holding this attitude helps to strengthen the essence of what we do.

# Chapter 12.
# Destiny Never Lets Go
## Sailing Back to the Source

*We are all like sons and daughters of a vineyard owner of staggering wealth and possessions. Everything that belongs to the vineyard owner also belongs to each son and daughter. Since each son and daughter has everything, they see the need to do nothing.*

*In time they become selfish and self-centered. The land owner has many vineyards to be managed and created, and he cannot do it all. Each day he watches his sons and daughters squander their talents on childish games instead of helping in the vineyard. One day he decides to take action. He sends the sons and daughters far away into a land with little comforts. Here there is a school to train them how to use their talents and develop their skills. Here they will learn to accept the challenges of life and polish the qualities of Soul by experience. The vineyard owner knows that one day they will return as masters of life, their talents no longer hidden behind foolish games. Each of them will become shining Souls, capable and effective. - Able to manage, expand and create new, wonderful and beautiful vineyards.*

This parable is actually very true about the divine nature of life, for a long time ago we were all in the pure positive worlds of heaven, but Soul became selfish, and self centered. No longer did Soul wish to serve.

It was only interested in foolish games. So the divine source, or God if you like, offered Soul the option of experiencing life through a coarser self. It would make life more difficult, but Soul could learn to master this lower self, and in doing so enable some of Soul's talents to come to the surface so more of Soul's qualities would shine. Soul was like the child stuck on a boat in the middle of a paddling pool without any oars. Although it loved splashing around in the pool, it also knew it needed help, and the condition of getting help was to learn how to row the boat.

So when each Soul was ready it accepted the first of the coarser vessels which is the Etheric body. Over time Soul learned how to master this body. The reward, as it were, was to go to a higher level of difficulty. So it next accepted the Mental body. Time passed and Soul mastered this body, then moved onto the Causal body, then the Astral body, and finally the highest level of difficulty, the Physical body.

This is where we are today. Time after time Soul returns to this physical realm to learn better ways of living and unfolding, and most of all **how to live life from the golden heart of Soul.**

## Spiritual Masters

There comes a point when Soul becomes the master of life. No longer does it need to return to this physical realm as it has become a co-worker with the divine source. It now chooses from the infinite worlds how to serve life. It is now the shining God Realized being. There are many people like this in the world, helping Souls on their way. They are not necessarily well known. They seek no recognition for their work. Their paths are silent, their work is great.

These are the Spiritual Masters who help all those Souls who require assistance spiritually in life. Some people see them as angels. They could even be the person who said a kind word to you on a street corner and it changed your life. Their mission in life is beyond the concept of most Souls, for these are the bold and adventuresome. Their spiritual strength is great, and their wisdom beyond measure. They move beyond the realms of time and dwell consciously in the higher worlds of Soul, while going about their daily missions here on Earth.

Whatever your mission in life is, it will usually extend beyond this physical region whether you are conscious of this or not. Some people think of the extent of life or creation as being contained on Earth, however, there are other worlds on this Physical Plane that contain life in varying forms.

Soul is infinite. It chooses whatever experiences it needs and where it will gain those experiences. On every level up through the Astral, Causal, Mental and Etheric

Planes, there are simply vast worlds beyond the comprehension of most. When we reach the Soul Plane we enter the regions of infinity. They all contain Souls expressing the divine spark of love.

Each of your inner vessels works as part of a team under the guidance of Soul to bring your mission about. You, as Soul, on the Soul Plane too, are carrying out the highest vision of this mission. So your mission in life not only makes a difference on this Physical Plane but in all of the divine worlds.

This level of activity with all of your bodies working as a team serving life will increase the momentum of spiritual growth. Within a period of time, depending on your state of consciousness, you may find yourself working within higher Soul Realized states of consciousness. It is from these regions that you begin to truly master life.

You will notice that as you move through each event, each situation, and each day it will be blessed by your presence. This is not some kind of energy that you direct, but the oceans of love within you flowing through each situation and event you move through.

It is not uncommon to begin to see the inner light. At first it may be like small spots of light, like stars, or it may be greater than this. You may even hear the celestial sounds of the inner worlds, like the rushing of winds, woodwind instruments, waterfalls, birds chirping or even indescribable sounds. These are all indications of your higher state of consciousness. You may notice moments when love simply pours out of your heart like a wave on a majestic ocean of light. This love touches the golden shores of every Soul.

**Ultimately, everything in life comes back to love. It is ever flowing out from the heart of the divine source. As long as we keep on moving with the spiritual flow of life we will fulfill our mission. It is our destiny, and destiny never lets go.**

In this physical realm we have a very limited degree of freedom. We have to haul this physical body along. We have to protect it from damage, feed it, and work within the constraints of time. Yet as we step up through each inner body, we find the restraints are much less. The mind on the Mental Plane, for instance, experiences a huge amount of freedom, but it is in Soul that we find ultimate freedom. That is why when we conceive of something from this Soul state it becomes life-changing and life-enhancing, beyond our wildest dreams. It is really only from this high state of consciousness that we can break old habits, and move beyond our barriers and limitations.

Your mission, your destiny is as the river. It flows from the heart of Soul back to the divine source, and in doing so it serves all of life. Destiny never lets go because whatever river we choose will always lead to Soul Realization and beyond.

If you use the HU song spiritual exercise on a daily basis you will begin to expand your consciousness beyond the limitations of these lower words, and into the exalted states of Soul Realization. From here you can literally become the conscious dreamer, serving life and flowing with the light of God.

You are never alone on your path as you have a spiritual guide at your side at all times. However, they never ever intrude or invade your space or privacy. These God

Realized beings will help and guide you only if you wish. **Their only concern is your spiritual progress.**

Many Souls have walked the path into Soul Realization before you, and of these many are ready to help those who follow. This is how they have chosen to serve life.

In closing I wish to say that love is very simple, and it is love that actually sets you free. It is not contained in rituals, doctrines, or beliefs, but in your heart. If you are free then you will by your very own nature set others free. In giving yourself the freedom to follow your mission in life, this too you do for others. Your very nature will become an inspiration to those who can see. **And your nature becomes that of Soul's golden heart**; infused with love, wisdom, spiritual power, courage, joy and divine light. - **Each of your qualities of Soul, polished to a sparkle, shining like ten thousand suns.**

It is from your heart that your true greatness emerges like a mighty ocean. It begins now with the brightest vision in the heart of Soul. Hold it close, absorb it, and follow it, for it will lead you to **untold spiritual riches.** This is your true inheritance, your true destiny in life, it is a gift that only you can open.

**I wish you every success in your mission. I know that you can succeed in catching the vision and finding your mission, simply because that is what you came into this world to do. May you experience many golden moments along the way.**

*With love*

*[signature]*

# General Information

## Purchasing Copies of This Book

Further copies of this book can be purchased from any of the International addresses listed on the next page.

Book Price:
Orders within USA and Canada $10.
Foriegn orders to the USA add $2 for Postage.

Orders within England £7.50.
Overseas orders add £2 for Postage.

Orders within Australia AU$15.
Overseas orders add AU$4 for Postage.

## Spiritual Poster

The front cover of this book is available as a large color wall poster. It was specially designed to illuminate the imagination, and is a great aide for quiet contemplation. The poster comes with a special set of twelve spiritual exercises to help you on your journey.

Cost is $5 within the **USA and Canada** including postage. Foriegn orders to the USA add $2 for postage.

For orders within **England** the cost is £4. Overseas orders to England should add £2 for postage.

For orders within **Australia** the cost is AU$8. Overseas orders to Australia should add AU$2 for postage.

## Winds of Destiny

This is a periodical newsletter, published at various times during the year. It has been specifically designed to help you with your special mission in life. The core of this newsletter takes an extended look at the various aspects of catching Soul's vision and finding your mission. Each issue contains readers letters sharing personal experiences, a number of spiritual exercises, and questions and answers. Plus various other topics and information on public workshops and talks around the world.

To receive this newsletter please write marking the envelope Winds of Destiny.

Yearly subscription $10 within the **USA and Canada**. Foriegn orders to the USA should add $2 for postage.

From **England** the cost is £7. Overseas orders to England should add £2 for postage

For orders within **Australia** the cost is AU$14. Overseas orders to Australia should add AU$2 for postage.

## Personal Letters

Some personal letters will be answered individually where time allows. Others, with your permission, will be answered via the Winds of Destiny newsletter. Please clearly mark the envelope Personal Letter. If you mark your letters Editor these will be reprinted in the quarterly journal where space and relevance allow.

## Audio Cassette

All the spiritual exercises mentioned in this book are available on this beautiful audio recording. It can benefit those who have trouble with concentration. However, try the exercises first as they are very easy.

Costs $6 within the the **USA and Canada**. Foriegn orders to the USA should add $2 for postage.

From **England** the cost is £4. Overseas orders to England should add £2 for postage.

For orders within **Australia** the cost is AU$8. Overseas orders to Australia should add AU$2 for postage.

## How to Pay for Items

Payment should be made to **"Bright Star"**.

### Within the USA and Canada
Please make payments within the USA and Canada with a personal check / money order in US dollars only.
### Foriegn orders to the USA
Please make payments with an international money order, made payable in US dollars.

### Orders within England
Please make payments by personal cheque /postal order.
### Overseas orders to England
Please make payments with an international money order, made payable in pounds sterling.

### Orders within Australia
Please make payments by personal cheque/money order.
### Overseas orders to Australia
Please make payments with an international money order, made payable in Australian dollars.

## International Addresses

Please use one of the following addresses for letters or when ordering:

**Bright Star**
c/o The Loving Heart Holistic Health Center
Post Office Box 1829
Carrollton, Georgia
30117-7129
**UNITED STATES OF AMERICA**

**Bright Star**
Mulberry House
53 Church Street
Weybridge
Surrey KT13 8DJ
**ENGLAND**

**Bright Star**
Post Office Box 5292
Albany
WA 6330
**AUSTRALIA**

## About The Loving Heart Holistic Health Center

The Loving Heart Holistic Health Center sells items through mail order that might assist and/or encourage people to live healthier daily lives. To request a mail order catalog and/or to request that your name, or your organization's name, be added to the Loving Heart Holistic Health Center's mailing list, please print your mailing address and/or e-mail address, and mail it to either the following e-mail address: lhhhc@lhhhc.com or the following mailing address: Loving Heart Holistic Health Center, Post Office Box 1829, Carrollton, Georgia, 30117-7129, U.S.A. The Loving Heart Holistic Health Center's Internet homepage address is: http://www.lhhhc.com